Praise for *The Philosophical Investor*

"Gary Carmell's honest, personal, and insightful account of how he and his partners have generated outsized returns for their investors over the course of thirty years is a must read—whether you are curious about simply making money, or the more complex challenge of living an honest, loving, and engaged life."

—**Willy Walker,** President/CEO, Walker & Dunlop

"Gary Carmell presents a very compelling investment discipline based upon strong underlying principles. All investors can learn from his ability to draw valuable perspective from many areas, including philosophy, music, history, and his own personal experiences. One of the most important foundations for investment success is a thirst for knowledge and understanding—Carmell is the epitome of this."

—**Timothy J. Ballard,** President, Buchanan Street Partners

"*The Philosophical Investor* is full of great investment advice and gives the reader many useful approaches to making financial decisions. It is truly a fun and inspiring read that will leave a lasting impression!"

—**Brian Stoffers,** Global President of
Debt & Structured Finance, CBRE

"Gary Carmell is analytical, independently minded, and meticulous in his investment approach. He is one of the first people from whom I would seek advice regarding US properties, and *The Philosophical Investor* is a must-read for investors interested in the US apartment sector."

—**Stephen Chung,** Managing Director,
Zeppelin Real Estate Analysis, Hong Kong

The

PHILOSOPHICAL

INVESTOR

TRANSFORMING

WISDOM

into WEALTH

GARY CARMELL

GREENLEAF
BOOK GROUP PRESS

Published by Greenleaf Book Group Press
Austin, Texas
www.gbgpress.com

Distributed by Greenleaf Book Group

For ordering information or special discounts for bulk purchases, please contact
Greenleaf Book Group at PO Box 91869, Austin, TX 78709, 512.891.6100.

Design and composition by Greenleaf Book Group
Cover design by Greenleaf Book Group
Cover image: ©istock/AndreaAstes

Publisher's Cataloging-In-Publication Data
Carmell, Gary.
    The philosophical investor : transforming wisdom into wealth / Gary Carmell.—First edition.
    pages : illustrations ; cm
    Issued also as an ebook.
    ISBN: 978-1-62634-169-2
    1. Carmell, Gary. 2. CWS Capital Partners (Firm) 3. Capitalists and financiers—Biography.
4. Investments—Philosophy. 5. Wealth—Philosophy. I. Title.

HG172.C37 A3 2015
332.6/092 2014947169

Part of the Tree Neutral® program, which offsets the number of trees consumed in
the production and printing of this book by taking proactive steps, such as planting
trees in direct proportion to the number of trees used: www.treeneutral.com

TreeNeutral®

Printed in the United States of America on acid-free paper

15 16 17 18 19 20   10 9 8 7 6 5 4 3 2 1

First Edition

To my father, Sherman Carmell (1930–1998).

Through your love and support you imparted wisdom, courage,
and how to live a truly wealthy life.
I miss you, Dad.

Acknowledgments

To Roneet: You are my best friend, a divine gift to all who are lucky to have you in their lives, a woman who radiates extraordinary beauty inside and out and makes me laugh like no one else, a mother beyond compare, and the only person with whom I have ever wanted to share this incredible roller coaster of life. You have imparted more wisdom than anyone else in my life. You have brought such abundance and wealth to our marriage and family. Here's looking at you, kid.

To Steve, Mike, and Bill: You are the best partners anyone could ever wish for. My life has been enhanced with your encouragement, support, and accountability. You have made coming to work every day so interesting, enjoyable, rewarding, and fun. There is no one else I would rather be holed up with in the heat of battle. Even during the darkest days, I knew we would persevere and prevail because our bonds were unbreakable, our commitment to our investors fearless and of paramount importance, and we'd been blessed with a CWS team giving it their all, knowing better days were ahead. And now that those better days are upon us, it is so rewarding to enjoy and share the fruits of our labor together.

To Jacob and Ariella: You are two amazing kids and I am so blessed to be your father. I am so proud of you and you have brought great joy into my life, even when you're fighting. I have always wanted to leave you with a legacy of some of my writings. Here it is . . . and maybe one day you'll even read it!

To the incredible CWS team that I have had the pleasure and honor of working with for so many years: You are some of my dearest friends, and you have made work a joy and added so much to my life. Thank you for all that you do. I am one very lucky man to have the pleasure of working with such a motley crew of talented, interesting, kind, and entertaining people. You're also a great-looking bunch too! I guess it is true that a company is a reflection of its leaders.

To Heidi at Guild West: I don't believe this book would have broken through the dream stage had it not been for your extraordinary encouragement and support over the many years we have worked together. I can unequivocally say that you have been my biggest fan.

To the team at Greenleaf: Thank you so much for taking a chance on me and the tremendous support you have shown me throughout the process.

To Mike and Steve (board members): Thank you so much for your extraordinary guidance, wisdom, and support over the many years you have been advising and cheering us on. You are the embodiment of the notion that a true friend is one who stabs you in the front. I want to particularly thank you for your help with this book.

And finally, to our loyal cadre of investors: Your incredible support and faith in CWS has made doing what I do so extraordinarily fulfilling. Thank you for the opportunity to do my small part in helping to grow wealth in your lives.

Contents

Part I

PREPARING *for the* MUNGER MOMENT

INTRODUCTION

The practical philosopher transforms ideas into life;
he acts, therefore, in a thoroughly reasonable manner;
he is consistent, regular, deliberate; he is never hasty or
passionate; he never allows himself to be influenced by the
impression of the moment. The theoretical philosopher enriches
the domain of reason by adding to it; the practical philosopher
draws upon it, and makes it serve him.
—Arthur Schopenhauer

I have worked in the world of investments for nearly thirty years with the same firm, CWS Capital Partners. Our focus has been in real estate, first manufactured housing communities (1969–1998) and then apartments beginning in 1988. We started winding down our emphasis on the former in the early 1990s as we began concentrating almost exclusively on the latter during the same period. While our focus on a particular industry may have been very specific versus that of a stock market investor deploying capital in many companies operating in a wide range of industries, I am confident that the lessons learned have been universal: applicable to any serious investor or thoughtful person who finds great rewards in following the advice of the Oracle of Delphi to "know thyself." Owning these businesses directly and controlling their cash flows and personnel decisions—rather than participating through passive ownership interests—has afforded us invaluable experience.

The most important lesson I have learned over my career is that "Shift Happens" (tectonic shift, that is) and that we can either monetize these shifts (increase wealth and/or vital experience) or let them inevitably monetize us (we lose money and/or take very little from the experience). Or, said differently, these shifts can catalyze tremendous personal growth (including financial growth) or be sources of great regression and stagnation if we don't rise to meet the challenges or if we were not able to avoid them in the first place.

I think of tectonic shifts as massive changes that alter the trajectory of an industry or one's life. Some can hit in an instant, like the earthquake and tsunami that decimated the Japanese nuclear energy industry virtually overnight in 2011. Such instant shifts can also be deeply personal, as when my son was two years old in 1995 and suffered a massive stroke, an event that has changed our family members' lives forever.

The more typical pattern, however, is for stresses to build up over time and then implode when the foundation can no longer hold. Examples of these include the subprime lending debacle (2002–2009) and, something that hit very close to home for my firm, the collapse of the manufactured housing industry after 1998. By anticipating tectonic shifts or having the resiliency to courageously respond to them with the appropriate action when they occur, the philosophical investor can generate great wealth and avoid significant losses.

Our lives are much like nature and the financial markets. Most of the time, they plod along from day to day with nothing out of the ordinary taking place. There are those rare times, however, when in an instant something transpires that can change the course and trajectory of our lives by impacting our physical well-being, our careers, our relationships, those we care for, or our financial resources. In some cases more than one of these will be impacted simultaneously. These tectonic shifts can be sources of great pain, suffering, frustration, and exasperation for those who find themselves ill prepared for the event or without the resilience to bounce back. At the same time, for the small minority that either anticipated it or can recover far ahead of the pack, such an event can represent tremendous opportunities and building blocks for greater strength, meaning, and wealth creation. As Epictetus said, "It's not what happens to you, but how you react to it that matters."

I have found that a philosophical framework is critical in helping me take a step back away from the cacophony of conventional wisdom and all of the corresponding "thou shalts" and to merge onto the proverbial road less traveled. Choosing this path not only suits my more solitary nature, but I believe it also improves my chances of identifying what tectonic shifts might be forming and when they may occur. I am more able to reflect and respond thoughtfully instead of reacting impulsively, creating more clarity and vision.

I do not want to give the impression, however, that I am immune to the same powerful psychological forces creating the prodigious blind spots and suboptimal decision making that most people fall prey to. This is not the case at all. Rather, I hope to show in this book where I have failed, the lessons learned from my mistakes, and how these lessons were subsequently reapplied much more successfully. The real education for the reader will come, I hope, from learning about the specifics of the journey, struggles, failures, successes, heartaches, and rewards.

As someone said to me once, it's better to be a meaningful specific than a wandering generality. It is my hope that the specifics of my journey will be far more interesting and informative than merely espousing general theories. I believe that only through experience, trial and error, and observation can we begin to discern patterns that can be formed into more general theories and postulates. This is a book that moves from micro to macro.

While most investment books are written with the complete benefit of hindsight, I have always been more fascinated by what decision makers were thinking in real time: in particular, what psychological forces they were up against in the face of imperfect information and powerful incentives and constraints. Unfortunately, with the possible exception of George Soros's *Alchemy of Finance*, I cannot think of many other books that take such an approach. One non-book that nevertheless provides a real-time source of deep, in-the-moment wisdom has been Warren Buffett's letters to his shareholders. I have read every one of them going back to 1956, and his writing style and what he communicates have been very influential to me over the years. I have been writing quarterly letters to our investors since the late 1990s as well as annual report letters and communications related to the specifics of individual investments within our portfolio. It is a large body of work, and this discipline has been quite helpful to me for organizing my thoughts to convey how we were viewing the environment at the time and to explain our outlook for the future. It also had the added benefit of going on record with our predictions, for which we could be held accountable. Equally important, these written communications have allowed us to go back and learn from our mistakes and successes.

Another one of my personal interests is to read old newspaper articles, particularly from the 1920s and 1930s. I see so many parallels between then and now, and these historical snapshots have helped me understand what was happening in real time, without hindsight bias. You will see how I relied heavily on this source material to help put the pieces of the puzzle together in the midst of the Great Recession to aid us in identifying what would happen with jobs, interest rates, real estate capitalization rates, and the growth in our operating income. This was hugely influential for us in terms of giving us the confidence that interest rates would not rise despite massive government spending, that jobs would materialize more quickly than most people thought, and that apartments were going to be very lucrative investments.

For most of us, the Great Recession was one of the most significant financial tectonic shifts in our lives, rocking the global economy and financial markets from 2007 through 2009 with the loss of trillions in wealth and millions of jobs. Although not immune to the negative effects of the worst downturn since the Great Depression, CWS was strong enough to be able to go on offense starting in late 2010 to embark on what we believed would be one of the greatest investment opportunities in a very long time. This book will show how we were prepared for this opportunity—one that I call a "Munger Moment," named after Charlie Munger, Warren Buffet's partner at Berkshire Hathaway (more about this later)—and took advantage of it.

Simplistically, I believe we at CWS are hypothesis generators in that we must have a reason or set of reasons as to why we think a particular investment will perform well over the years. After we make the purchase it is then up to us to keep testing the hypotheses and monitoring the results to see if our premises were accurate or flawed. It is my intention with this book to tap into some of the material I wrote in the past along with my current thoughts to show what we were thinking and the decisions we were making when it came to anticipating and/or reacting to some very powerful tectonic shifts. These decisions included

- exiting the manufactured housing business between 1998 and 2000, just prior to its long-term collapse;

- transitioning into the apartment business at a time when single-family home demand was exploding and the demand for rentals was diminishing;

- making a terrible decision to use fixed-rate financing with cost-prohibitive prepayment penalties at a time when interest rates were dropping and revenues were declining, and subsequently having to ask our investors to put more money into their investments;

- navigating through the subprime debacle and anticipating its impact on our apartment business;

- capitalizing on an extraordinary opportunity for apartment investors to capture the tremendous rewards accruing to those taking advantage of the transition to more of a renter nation (CWS's Munger Moment); and

- dramatically changing our financing strategy to emphasize variable-rate loans: why we did this, and the financial benefits that we have reaped as a result.

I also intend to convey how important partnering with extraordinary individuals has been in all aspects of my life. I am convinced that the tremendous gifts and abundance that have been bequeathed to me would not have materialized had I not been blessed with my business partners Steve Sherwood, Bill Williams, and Mike Engels and a life partner beyond compare in my wife Roneet. Through these partnerships we have collectively been able to anticipate and/or react to powerful tectonic shifts that have generated tremendous growth for CWS, for my family, as well as for me personally. These include the aforementioned strategic decisions we made with our business to exit one form of real estate prior to its implosion and enter into another more lucrative area that has paid tremendous dividends for our investors. And from a personal perspective, the experience my wife and I had regarding my son's stroke and a lifetime of residual issues, the unconventional decision we made with regard to our daughter's schooling, and two important investment decisions that were personal Munger Moments for us have been deeply impactful tectonic shifts in our lives. They have resulted in us crying together, strategizing with one another, thinking creatively, laughing, taking risks, enjoying immense rewards, and living a deeply interesting and fulfilling life that has been a fascinating journey for which I look back in amazement and awe. I am one lucky person to have such a beautiful, smart, canny, and insightful woman leading the charge in our relationship and for our family.

I will also show why I think apartments still offer a wonderful investment opportunity for a number of years to come, some of the ways to evaluate whether an investment management firm is right for you, and what Shakespeare has taught me about knowing myself and others. The books ends on a personal, philosophical note that highlights some of my reflections on what constitutes true wealth—much of which is not strictly financial in nature.

This is a story about a unique individual (that would be me: a legend in my own mind!) and an extraordinary firm, CWS Capital Partners, which over the course of nearly thirty years has grown from approximately $250 million in assets in one form of real estate—manufactured housing communities—to over $3.0 billion in another—apartments. During this time together we have done hundreds of transactions when accounting for property purchases, sales, refinances, recapitalizations, and loan restructures (yes, we have had our challenges). We were able to avoid losses in our manufactured housing and apartment investments while generating annual returns in excess of 13 percent compounded, after accounting for all fees for the apartment communities we have sold. This represents a total of 55 properties (approximately $1.5 billion in value) sold since 1996, as of this writing.

In addition, real estate has some unique tax advantages from which our investors have benefitted. We almost always utilize tax-deferred exchanges when we sell a property. This allows investors to roll over their appreciated investments without having to pay tax, affording them much more pre-tax wealth at work than the equivalent stock market investor who would pay capital gains taxes on the profit and then reinvest after-tax proceeds in the next investment. Further, if the investors don't ever need to sell, their heirs inherit the asset at the market value upon the investors' death. All of the deferred taxes accrued due to the depreciation (a noncash expense) that sheltered some of the income and distributions received over the years are now eliminated. It's a pretty powerful wealth preservation tool that will be quantified later with a very interesting and compelling example from the results of one of our investors. I also happen to appreciate it, since the bulk of my net worth is represented by real estate.

I have not only had incredible partners in business and in life—including my wife of twenty-five years (as of this writing), who has more common sense and gumption than anyone I know—but some amazing sages as well, most of whom I have never met. These include the thoughts and writings of a number of brilliant philosophers, investors, economists, writers, and songwriters. This is why I have applied to this book the subtitle *Transforming Wisdom into Wealth*. The phrase is a reference to alchemy and the philosopher's stone, that elusive tool said to transform lead into gold, life into eternal youth, flaws into perfection.

I have always been fascinated by finding patterns in numbers and connecting seemingly unrelated events. I have used such connections to form unconventional insights that help us stay off the mountain while the conditions for an avalanche are forming. They also help us find the courage to get back on while lift tickets are being dramatically discounted because so many skiers are still digging themselves out and the owners of the resort are under great financial pressure.

The first rule of investing is to avoid situations where one is at great risk of losing one's capital permanently. One is then free to focus on the rewards. During times of uniform investor euphoria, it is imperative for investors to pay attention when disastrous conditions are forming. If they are unable or unwilling to do so, then they should try to have their money with those who are. Devastating losses, which may never be recouped, can result for those who become complacent or stay at the party too long.

The NASDAQ is still below 5,000, nearly fifteen (as of this writing) years after reaching its peak in March 2000, while the Nikkei is more than 60 percent lower than it was in 1989. These events represent financial avalanches in which those who bought at the top are still digging themselves out. Investing has taught me the importance of avoiding catastrophic error in all aspects of life, and the most important way of doing this is by ruthlessly analyzing our contribution to past errors and where we are most susceptible to self-delusion or manipulation by others.

By tapping into such brilliant people as nineteenth-century philosopher Arthur Schopenhauer, Shakespeare, famed investor Charlie Munger, mythologist Joseph Campbell, economist John Maynard Keynes, legendary investors Warren Buffett and John Templeton, brilliant journalist and writer Walter Lippmann, Nobel Prize–winning physicist Richard Feynman, hedge fund titan George Soros, Jim Rogers (Soros's former partner), Bob Dylan, Depression-era Federal Reserve chairman Marriner Eccles, and iconoclastic investor, inventor, and economic theorist Warren Mosler, just to name some of the more influential, I have been able to think more independently, learn from my mistakes, better anticipate tectonic shifts, and be able to find meaning even when devastating events take place. In short, I have gradually been able to transform wisdom into wealth.

One day, as I was looking through my library, I became curious as to why I was far more interested in people who have been long departed from this world than those who are still living. Lo and behold, I found the answer from Schopenhauer, who, on the subject of mentors, has been quoted as saying:

> Talent hits a target no one can hit. Genius hits a target no one else can see.

He goes on to say in *The World As Will and Idea, Volume II*:

> The very stamp which genius impresses upon its works is that their excellence is unfathomable and inexhaustible. Therefore they do not grow old, but become the instructor of many succeeding centuries. The perfected masterpiece of a truly great mind will always produce a deep and powerful effect upon the whole human race, so much so that it is

impossible to calculate to what distant centuries and lands its enlightening may extend.

If ideas can stand the test of time and have relevance throughout the ages, then these are what I'm most interested in, and the geniuses who formulated them are who I want to partner with, in addition to my business associates and my wife. Their ideas are so powerful that I believe effectively utilizing them and applying them when and where appropriate can substantially improve the odds of success in the world of investing, as I hope to show in this book.

I'm proud of what we have accomplished at CWS and even more excited about the prospects for the future. The apartment industry is well positioned for long-term growth, in my opinion. Our results did not happen by accident, although I will admit we have definitely had our share of amazing luck over the years. I intend to show what formative experiences, tectonic events, and key partnerships have taught me. I also want to highlight the ways that I have applied the wise counsel of geniuses from multiple disciplines in order to transform wisdom into wealth. I hope to show how this training has positioned CWS and me to take advantage of Munger Moments by seizing those rare opportunities when the odds have been strongly in our favor and all we needed were the resources and courage to take advantage of them. Munger Moments are rare, but when recognized and acted on, they can radically alter the financial and emotional resources available to the individual or business that seizes them. Noted comparative religion and mythology expert Joseph Campbell, another key influence in my life and this book, said in an interview:

> There will be a moment when the walls of the world seem to open for a second and you get an insight through. Jump then! Go! The gates will often close so fast that they take off the tail of your horse. You may be dismembered, lose everything you have.

This is a good depiction of how fleeting these life-altering opportunities may be. They can be terribly frightening, but not acting can be more devastating than putting all of one's heart and soul into taking the plunge. Interestingly, however, Munger indicates that with enough intellectual and psychological preparation (greater self-awareness) these moments can actually offer immense rewards with relatively little risk. I hope to show you how some of these Munger Moments have shown up for me personally and professionally, how they were recognized as such, the actions that were taken, and the rewards generated. The best way to describe a Munger Moment is to use his own words. Munger said the following:

> Our experience tends to confirm a long-held notion that being prepared, on a few occasions in a lifetime, to act promptly in scale, in doing some simple and logical thing, will often dramatically improve the financial results of that lifetime.

> A few major opportunities, clearly recognizable as such, will usually come to one who continuously searches and waits, with a curious mind that loves diagnosis involving multiple variables.

> And then all that is required is a willingness to bet heavily when the odds are extremely favorable, using resources available as a result of prudence and patience in the past.

This is powerful stuff and probably requires multiple readings to get its true essence. Philosophers over millennia have tried to describe nirvana, that state of enlightenment where people can live from their unique and authentic quiet centers. From an investment perspective, I have been in constant search of nirvana, and I think I finally discovered it with the help of Munger's extraordinary description. When everything lines up as

Munger describes, that, to me, is nirvana for an investor and embodies everything I have tried to work for:

- preparation
- macro analysis
- evaluation of risk/reward to know when the odds are in your favor
- patience and independent thinking that allows for sidestepping the problems that everyone else fell prey to
- access to capital
- courage to take the necessary action to capitalize on the opportunity

In addition to my belief about the power of tectonic shifts and their ability to make or break us, I also have strong beliefs about how investors are often their own worst enemies. I recall a seminar I was attending a number of years ago. The presenter that day asked us to sum up our business in a sentence that would be so captivating that the other party would have to know more about what we do. When it came time for me to share, I said, "We help save people from themselves." He asked if we were in the ministry business. After a quick chuckle I said, "No, we're a real estate investment firm."

He didn't make the connection, but he also wanted to know more. I explained that most human beings are not wired to be good investors, because they are much more comfortable being part of a crowd as opposed to being on the outside looking in. This can be a fatal flaw and the main reason why most of us find investing to be quite frustrating at times. Such an attitude usually results in emotional decisions that lead us to buy at the top (when everyone is most euphoric) and sell at the bottom (when things look the worst, and the opportunities are the best). I intend to delve into some of the psychological blind spots that get in the way of making better investment decisions.

Although I am a Chartered Financial Analyst (CFA) and follow financial markets fairly closely, my practical experience over the years has been in real estate. As I have previously mentioned, virtually all of my net worth is in real estate. One may question the applicability of my experience to anyone reading this book that doesn't make real estate investments regularly, since these investments tend to be made less frequently and are far less liquid than marketable securities. Yet, that is one of the great benefits of real estate as a learning laboratory. It typically requires investors to be far more thoughtful and discerning (except during the subprime debacle) when it comes to making such an investment because of the illiquid nature, the relatively high transaction costs, the complexity, and other factors.

Real estate also often requires asking important questions like, "Why do I think this property or location will be more valuable over time?" "What are the economic, social, and demographic forces that may influence this investment?" "Have I consulted with the appropriate experts to thoroughly evaluate the risks?" "Can I truly afford losing money on this investment?" "Have I picked the best leverage (loan) strategy for this particular asset and my personal risk tolerance?" And the list goes on and on. Because it is time consuming and costly to get in and out of real estate investments, much thought should be put into them. The stock market, however, is so liquid, and we can get such instant feedback on the change in value of our investments that we become brutally prone to powerful psychological forces that prey on our faulty neurological and psychological wiring.

It has been said that markets are designed to create the greatest amount of harm to the greatest number of people. They are able to do this because of the potential for everyone to be leaning in the same direction in the boat, causing it to tip over. Liquid markets can overwhelm us with information, and our world of the Internet, Twitter, and Facebook can stir up the masses more quickly than at any time in history when there is a perception of easy money to be made or great risk of loss. This information overload is the catalyst to get everyone to lean in the same direction, which, according to my philosophy on investing, is precisely where you don't want to be.

While the opportunities chronicled in this book are somewhat unique to CWS and me personally, they are varied. In other words, there are always going to be game-changing opportunities, whether they be in the investment arena, the home we buy, the life partner we choose, the job we take, the person we meet, or anything else. The opportunities are boundless. By sharing the specifics of this journey, including the preparation, trials, and in-depth analysis, my intention is to help influence the mindset of the reader. If one accepts the premise that life is always providing opportunities, then individuals, couples, families, and firms need to cultivate an open mind, a deep-seated curiosity, an optimistic bias, the ability to think independently, the discipline to tie oneself to the mast when the siren call of easy money becomes so alluring (wisdom), and a willingness to take action when the opportunity presents itself (courage). Cultivating courage and wisdom takes training, but when they are effectively put into action our lives can make a quantum leap into a whole new evolved state that offers rewards we could only dream of previously.

I believe that I have found, or actually stumbled onto, a career (more about this later) that is perfectly suited for how I am wired. I am one of the lucky ones who has seen the advantages of moving away from the crowd. I have grown enormously, taken on new challenges, used my gifts in ways that are highly valued, made a difference in many people's lives, provided for my family, met interesting people, and built cherished lifetime relationships with my partners and coworkers. As Schopenhauer said, "The man who is born with a talent which he is meant to use, finds his greatest happiness in using it."

I am one of the fortunate ones. It's now time to talk about how I got to where I am today and the amazing company I have been associated with since 1987.

Chapter One

LEARNING TO PLAY THE GAME

You have to learn the rules of the game.
And then you have to play better than anyone else.
—*Albert Einstein*

As a young kid I was always fascinated by puzzles and statistics. I even created an elaborate dice baseball game where I would spend hours filling out scorecards on the results of the dice and then calculating the stats for the season. I was obsessed with baseball batting averages, earned run averages, and slugging percentages. I realized that within data, powerful relationships exist that can be used to make predictions or provide more clarity about the future. Numbers could talk to me if I could just be patient enough to listen and see. What I was really doing, I later recognized, was looking for patterns. The parallels with the world of investing should be obvious. Being in the real estate business—where we manage multiple properties in various cities—provides me with significant financial and operating data to draw from to establish some baseline operating metrics. These allow me to develop some fairly reliable rules of thumb to apply to the evaluation of new investments, and I can use these as a reality check on the investment assumptions we're making.

I've come to look back on my own personal journey and realize that it has often been a search for clues and a way to put the pieces of the puzzle together to form a mosaic that will unfold in a more clear picture. And as that picture unfolds, it becomes a little easier to put the rest of the pieces in place to make decisions about what to go for and what to avoid. I think all of this is designed to build up the muscles of courage and wisdom.

As I think back upon my school years, I recall that most children were given things to learn or were handed syllabi containing the list of reading materials, the due dates for the assignments, the topics for the tests, and so forth. That was kind of like leading the horse to water. But that's not the case in the real world, especially in investing. To succeed there involves a process of discovery, trial and error, and hypothesis testing. It requires a level of open-mindedness, humility, and confidence.

In investing, it's important to understand where information that could be the next clue to how people react and what their reaction functions are comes from. As humans, we're basically reaction machines; that can create tremendous opportunity and a lot of risk. I found that by taking a multidisciplinary approach to tapping into so many different types of information sources—particularly philosophers, dead economists, newspaper articles, psychology, and history—I had a way to figure out how to actually play the game of investing (and life). It was not unlike how you might play chess. Eventually the rules, patterns, and observations began unfolding for me, sometimes in very unusual ways. That allowed me to look at the world differently than others and formulate a divergent view of how things might turn out.

Finding My Path

When I headed west in 1983 to go to college at UCLA I didn't know what I wanted to do for a career. But I knew what I didn't want to do: become a lawyer. My father was a terrific lawyer, just like his father before him. My brother became a lawyer (although he didn't practice), and I have three brothers-in-law and a sister-in-law who are attorneys.

But despite my father's success and my family history, it just didn't seem to me to be a very appealing lifestyle to be at the beck and call of clients; I figured it would be better to be the client than the lawyer. What I did appreciate, however, was how skilled a writer my dad was and how much pride and effort he put into honing his craft. He wrote a lot of briefs, which were vitally important in helping him to put his thoughts down on paper in an organized, logical, and persuasive manner so that he had the highest probability of prevailing. He was quite successful, the highlight of his career being a unanimous victory in front of the Supreme Court that I had the pleasure of witnessing as a thirteen-year-old kid in 1978.

Although I didn't want to be a lawyer, I ironically chose a major that is typically very common for future lawyers: political science. I had very little aptitude for science. I was a decent math student but got my butt kicked in calculus (I never understood the reason for it even existing until I got to business school and did a deeper dive into statistics; I'm sure Newton and Einstein had some other important uses for it as well). I knew I would not head down either of those roads. Alas, I was faced with no choice but to delude myself that there was huge value in being a liberal arts major, despite having no intention of being lawyer. I told myself that I could always learn business by getting an MBA (UCLA didn't have a business degree program at that time) and that it would be best if I could get a broad education and really focus on improving as a writer. Little did I know that fate had some surprises in store for me as well.

Discovering My Financial Mentors

I delved into political science at UCLA as well as the broad general education curriculum that was required at the time. While I was never a reader growing up, I took a literature course in my freshman year and became hooked on reading, for which I'll forever be grateful (though the late nights spent turning pages have sometimes been a bane to my wife). My daughter has been an avid reader since age eight or so, but my son is more like I was pre-college. I was hoping the reading bug might hit him at some point but the odds are not in his favor, as you will come to learn later in the book. I also think it's very difficult in our digitally addicted age to develop the muscles of concentration enough to be able to sit down, focus, and enjoy a book. This skill typically needs to be cultivated at a younger age, although I was an exception.

At UCLA, I took some economics, accounting, and statistics classes and found myself enjoying them quite a bit. I remember reading recently an excerpt of a presentation that famed investor Howard Marks gave at Wharton. He highly recommended that those who wanted to go into the world of investing and who possessed a desire to distinguish themselves from competitors should polish their writing skills. Marks said, "You can get a lot of favorable attention when the recommendations that you submit are well framed and well argued." Interestingly, in the same interview he talked about how Wharton (the business school of the University of Pennsylvania, his alma mater) in the 1960s required students to take a course in foreign literature. He chose Japanese literature, and he said it changed his life. It transformed him into a very serious student and helped contribute deeply to his philosophy as an investor, particularly accepting that change is inevitable and there is nothing you can do to alter this. One either has to adapt or be made irrelevant. I'm a big fan of rock lyrics, so for me, Bob Dylan conveys the same message, but in a more powerful way: "He not busy being born is busy dying."

The bull market on Wall Street was really coming into force in 1985 and continued through my graduation in June 1987; this opened my eyes to the possibility of going into finance or business. I found myself increasingly following the financial news, especially the buyout mania financed by Michael Milken's high-yield team at Drexel Burnham, close by in Beverly Hills. I read and was fascinated by what Milken had accomplished and by his incredible mind, vision, and unwavering intensity and focus. I was getting hooked, and my deepening interest and growing curiosity fostered the desire to learn more. I wanted to study the greatest investors and learn how they made their money.

I began my studies with the master communicator and unparalleled investor Warren Buffett. I read every annual shareholder letter he wrote. Mind you, this was before the Internet and required me to contact the company to have them all sent to me. I thought I had died and gone to heaven! What an education! Not only were the letters chock-full of investing wisdom, but he was a good writer, too. He took complex subjects and material and made them accessible to anyone who took the time to read his letters. He also had a very personal, humble, and whimsical style that was quite engaging and made the letters flow quite smoothly. Buffett taught me the importance of communicating thoroughly and accessibly, giving your investors credit for being able to handle sophisticated material.

I don't remember the exact order of the influences who followed Buffett, but I eventually expanded my reach to George Soros and was mesmerized by his book *The Alchemy of Finance*. Based on his trading diary, the book captures his thought processes during a year in which, to the best of my recollection, his fund gained in excess of 100 percent based on his bet that oil prices would collapse and that the US dollar would strengthen dramatically. His book was extremely influential because it is obviously very easy to explain something with the benefit of 20/20 hindsight. But to be able to know what an investor was thinking and why he made the decisions he did using imperfect information as events were unfolding, overlaid with all of the psychological traps of self-doubt and overconfidence, makes it easier to assess whether his outcomes were influenced more by luck or by skill. Bill Williams, one of the founders of CWS, loves to quote Desiderius Erasmus: "In the kingdom of the blind, the one-eyed man is king." I never forget the importance of this.

Soros convinced me of the power and discipline of laying what you're thinking on the line in real time in a comprehensive manner, of taking action as a result of your conclusions. Indeed, only those managers who take this risk and open themselves up to looking foolish actually offer their investors a true gauge of who is investing their precious capital.

Soros's theory of *reflexivity* was also hugely influential on me; I came to learn that one cannot divorce the observer from the observed when it comes to investing. Said differently, if influential investors or lenders, particularly lenders, have a bullish inclination, then this will lead to the deployment of more capital in that particular sector or industry, which will then raise asset values and allow for more people to borrow against these elevated collateral values. That, in turn, leads to more investment and more lending, until the process reaches an unsustainable trajectory where lenders are lending almost entirely against future projections rather than based on current cash flow and values. Once they realize what has happened, the entire scenario reverses itself. Recognizing the power of reflexivity had a great impact on me when it came to studying the nature of investment bubbles. One can make a lot of money on the way up, riding the rising tide, but then it becomes critical to get out of the water when the tide goes out and capital is at great risk of being permanently lost.

The housing market offers a perfect example of this "reflexive" thinking. When people find that interest rates have come down and they don't have much confidence for investing in the stock market, they tend to buy housing more aggressively, thereby pushing values up. As these values go up, people are able to borrow against this higher value by taking out home equity loans or new mortgages with a higher loan balance. The homeowners then take the additional dollars and put them back into the housing market. This has the effect of pushing up home values even more. Meanwhile on the lending side, the lenders believe they are making relatively safe investments. After all, they are getting good rates of return as homes keep going up in value even as their risk goes down (because they have lent against appreciating assets). But what they ignore or don't even realize is the effect of their own behavior in this process. The mere act of lending aggressively (even when apparently prudent) is influencing what is observed. Appreciating collateral values give them more confidence to put more money into this industry, which further improves collateral values in a self-reinforcing cycle.

At some point something gives, and the economy turns down. Consumers or homeowners borrow too much. Cracks begin to occur in the credit quality of the loans or of the borrowers themselves, and as these cracks occur, lending standards begin to tighten up. Credit becomes either more costly or less accessible. This very act influences the purchasing power of homebuyers and impacts housing values negatively. It takes homes longer to sell, and those sellers who were reluctant to sell for a lower price eventually have no choice due to some catalytic event such as death, divorce, or debt. As the prices begin to drop, more recent sales become less supportive of prices paid by many buyers toward the top of the cycle. In turn, appraisers are influenced by these more recent transactions, lenders follow suit, and the declining price trend causes the cycle to lurch downward, with a corresponding decline in collateral values. As lenders start to tighten up and require more collateral to lend against, values are pushed lower as buying power is diminished, higher down payments are required, and stricter credit requirements remove marginal borrowers from the buying pool. George Soros's reflexive process postulates that market participants oftentimes don't realize that they are key actors in the equation, influencing their own worldviews in ways they don't understand.

It is so important to learn that you can view the world through more than one lens and that the lens that you look through can affect the very thing you are looking at. You need an inventory of different lenses, and you need the flexibility and the tools to know when and how to change lenses. Looking at life through a single lens will ultimately lead to bad decision making.

George Soros's partner Jim Rogers was also very influential in terms of helping me realize how important getting the "macro environment" right can be. Many value investors don't focus on this and prefer to let valuations guide them on the timing of an investment. I respect this greatly, but I do believe that in order to assess the longer-term earning power of a company or property, one has to make some assumptions about future demand trends and competition. For example, one could have bought manufactured housing companies after shipments dropped 50 percent, thinking they were at a bottom, only to find them dropping another 80 percent—representing a cumulative drop of over 90 percent from the peak—because they missed how devastating it can be for an industry when financing dries up and underwriting standards are permanently tightened. They would have lost a ton of money.

*   *   *

Now that you know a bit about how I'm wired, what I'm interested in, and the major influences on my investment philosophy and decisions, it's now time to tell you the interesting story about how I got my job at CWS back in 1987.

Chapter Two

THE PATH FROM THERE TO HERE

Life to me is a journey—you never
know what may be your next destination
—David Russell

It's fascinating to look back and see how my journey has unfolded, both as a person and as an investor. I've owned six homes and lost money on one of them. When I started working at CWS Capital Partners (previously Clayton, Williams & Sherwood, Inc.) in 1987, we owned properties in Texas at a time when Texas was going through a depression. I had to talk to equally depressed investors about the dire investment environment. But things got better, and now as president of CWS I have the pleasure of working with two amazing individuals: Steve Sherwood and Mike Engels. Along the way I have worked for two people—Bill Williams and Steve Sherwood—whose intuition, intelligence, and courage to take action were second to none. I enjoyed tremendous success with them, while also witnessing the collateral damage of seeing a number of my friends laid off and moving on to other careers. Oftentimes these experiences have led to better subsequent situations for those whose careers ended prematurely at CWS. Seeing them land on their feet and oftentimes in better-suited and rewarding positions has helped me to look for and find the long-term benefits from short-term, devastating tectonic shifts that can rock people's lives.

It's also interesting to look back and reflect on the series of decisions that led me into the forest and down the path that eventually resulted in me joining CWS. It all began back at UCLA, where I met my wife, Roneet. When I graduated, a year after she did, I joined her at her home in Orange County, about fifty miles south, rather than moving back to my home city of Chicago. It was a condition of us staying together, you see. I didn't know anyone in Orange County, but I did know that I wanted to manage stocks and bonds, so my wife suggested that I walk around the Fashion Island business and shopping area, dropping off my résumé at various investment firms as I went. My first stop was at an investment management firm called Clayton, Williams & Sherwood. The receptionist at CWS confirmed that the firm might indeed be hiring, so I left my résumé with her with a note that read, "Interested in a financial analyst position."

Upon subsequently visiting a few more businesses, I realized the futility and humiliation of trying to get a job this way. But a week later I got a call from CWS (hardly remembering who they were) inviting me for an interview. I asked them what they did again, and they said real estate. I said that I had always wanted to be in real estate, and gladly accepted the opportunity to be interviewed. I eventually got the job, but it's a little more interesting than that.

Bret was my first boss. He was completely dismissive of my liberal arts degree and asked if my plan when I chose that major was to open up a political science store. He had me sit down and teach myself the Lotus 1-2-3 spreadsheet computer program from a book. I designed spreadsheets and learned how the CWS acquisition models worked. At the time, CWS was one of the largest owner/operators of mobile home parks in the country: definitely a niche business, but a very lucrative one.

Paul was Bret's boss, and he later told me that he chose me over another candidate because I went to UCLA whereas the other guy went to USC. Oh, and I was taller and willing to work for less money. Much later, after I had achieved some level of success, he changed his tune and said he saw something in me that showed great potential!

After I started at CWS, the company began experiencing immense challenges in its prodigious mobile home park portfolio, particularly those properties located in Texas. Prior to 1986, the tax laws allowed passive real estate investors to offset any losses from their real estate holdings against their ordinary wages from their "real" jobs. Because real estate is usually a leveraged investment (debt is used to help finance the purchase) and typically is depreciated for tax purposes at rates greater than the annual capital expenditures spent to maintain the property, these "losses" are only on paper. Thus, distributions from these investments could not only be sheltered from taxes in the short run, but from a tax standpoint they could generate losses to reduce one's wage and salary income. Needless to say, this was a pretty good deal and led to a tremendous amount of capital coming into real estate. Not surprisingly, real estate syndication firms sprouted up to aggregate this capital, and by the mid-1980s there were huge dollars flowing into real estate. Texas was the epicenter of this.

Unfortunately, the party couldn't last forever, and the tax law change of 1986 was the first domino to fall. This eliminated the ability of investors to write off passive losses against active income, and now passive losses could only be used to offset passive income, with any unused amounts deferred until future years.

Texas was ground zero for fraudulent savings and loans that were often owned by real estate developers who would borrow 100 percent (if not more) of the development costs from their own S&Ls. For a period of time this growth made sense; Texas benefited greatly from the oil boom that took place in the 1970s and early 1980s. However, the confluence of way too much unsophisticated money aggregated by financial operators, fraudulent S&Ls run by crooked developers, and collapsing oil prices created a perfect storm of supply and demand imbalance for real estate owners. Just as demand was starting to wither, a ton of real estate supply was coming on that had been capitalized in the prior couple of years by all of the easy syndicator money.

At about this same time, 1986 or so, CWS and its investors became the owners of Creekside, which was a parcel of land in the Dallas area upon which a mobile home park was going to be built by CWS. It turned out to be a terrible time to embark on such a venture for the reasons just mentioned. The Texas economy was tanking as a result of these factors. So we had to bring in additional capital from our investors, and ultimately we negotiated a deal with the bank to write down its loan from $6 million to $3 million in exchange for a $2 million payment from us. Things were pretty bleak, but this turned out to be the darkness before the dawn. As the economy improved, we increasingly had the right debt burden and sufficient reserves to fill the vacant spaces and produce positive cash flow. We were able not only to break even, but also to make very large distributions to our patient investors. This is a good representation of how volatile our manufactured housing investments had become. It took a long time to get to that point: approximately seven years.

What a roller coaster ride it turned out to be. Our investors had benefited from extraordinary returns since the inception of the firm; previously, they had oftentimes received a multiple of their original investment from refinances of properties on very, very aggressive loan terms. Certainly, none of them ever expected to have to put money back in that they had pulled out. Unfortunately, the market had different plans. Occupancies started to drop as job losses led to a reduction in demand at a time when new properties were offering aggressive move-in incentives. Cash flow turned negative, and capital was needed to support these investments. I had a Paul McCartney and Wings moment when I said to myself: "If we ever get out of here, I'm going to figure out what went wrong so we can avoid it in the future."

Yet we hung in there, and we ended up selling the property for approximately $21 million in 1999, more than tripling our investors' money from all distributions. It was a huge turnaround that proved the importance of perseverance and capital access during tough times, so as to be there when the sun starts shining again.

As the carnage was unfolding in real estate, we also saw very compelling opportunities unfolding as a result of this massive liquidation, and we thought we could make money in apartments. After all, it wasn't a great leap from mobile home parks to apartments.

The same investors that we were asking for money to support their currently overleveraged, negatively cash-flowing mobile home park investments we now asked to take a leap of faith to back us in buying apartments. We also used money from the sale of mobile home parks in California, which we thought were overvalued due to an inflated real estate market and an economy reliant upon defense spending (soon to collapse after the fall of the Berlin Wall). We reinvested these proceeds into Texas apartments. From 1990 onward, we slowly divested ourselves of mobile home parks, and we redeployed the capital into apartments. The culmination of this was the sale in 1998 of virtually our entire mobile home park business and property portfolio, with an agreement that we had two years to redeploy the funds into apartments (more on this later).

It turned out to be great timing to get out of mobile home parks, because the industry collapsed as a result of terrible lending practices. Shipments of new mobile homes fell from approximately 373,000 in 1998 to only about 60,000 (as of this writing) at a time when apartments continued to do well.

As you now know, I'm a guy who likes to find patterns, particularly ones that can act as leading indicators. It eventually occurred to me that construction should be taking place to support underlying business growth and household formations but should not be the driver of the economy. In other words, we should not be building for the builders. I started messing around with job data and the composition of the employment base and decided to look at one very simple indicator: construction employment as a percentage of total non-farm employment. Boy, did this explain a lot in terms of helping me avoid similar avalanches that might occur in the future!

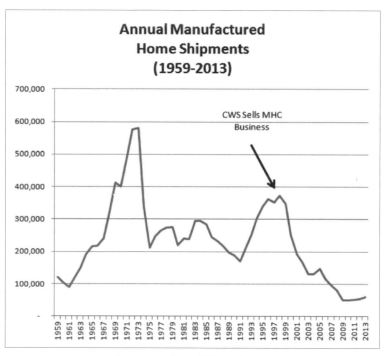

Source: Manufactured Housing Institute

Soros's partner Jim Rogers has been pretty adept at identifying excess optimism and pessimism throughout various industries over the years. I remember reading an interview with him once where he said that Donald Trump was bankrupt, but he didn't realize it yet—a fact that soon came to light. Rogers was also a strong advocate of getting out and seeing the world in order to let go of our American biases. He also believed that having a diverse educational background would improve one's odds of assimilating data from many industries and opportunities. He thought this made one more perceptive of risks that may exist outside of the United States and how these trends may impact US markets: something I hope that I am helping prove true.

Lessons from the Past

I love timeless wisdom from great minds of the past. In particular, I am drawn to those who have tried to learn from past mistakes or to think in a different way than the crowd. For instance, Michael Milken once asked why it took Canadians to see the value in New York City real estate when the city was on the verge of bankruptcy in the late 1970s. Why did it take a Saudi prince to see the value of Citicorp in the early 1990s, and why was the world's greatest investor located in Omaha and not New York City?

Indeed, people can be too close to a situation. I know that was a problem for us in terms of missing much of the real estate boom in our home state of California in the mid-1990s (we made many, many offers, but only bought one property), yet we were able to be aggressive buyers of Texas real estate after the implosion of the savings and loan industry and the creation of the Resolution Trust Corporation (RTC) to help clean up the mess.

As I looked for answers for how we might be able to avoid similar mistakes in the future, I came across the writings and various interviews of John Templeton. He lived in the Bahamas and found it extraordinarily valuable to be so far away from the emotional noise of Wall Street and other money centers around the world. I learned to admire him greatly for his deep spirituality, his philanthropy, and his lifestyle choice designed to cultivate the maximum amount of serenity and independent thinking. He would swim in the ocean every morning and focused on living a full and connected life. These all contributed to his being one of the greatest investors the world has ever seen. He would load the boat when fear and pessimism were at extremes and unload it when optimism and euphoria reigned. This is of course easier said than done, but it is much easier for someone who is out of the fray in the Bahamas versus someone stuck in the center of a hurricane of emotion, testosterone, and career-obsessed participants on Wall Street.

I also love the fact that Templeton lived through the Great Depression and took advantage of the bargains that materialized out of the carnage. I have a fascination for the 1920s and 1930s, so I am particularly interested in people who lived through those periods. They lived through the highest of the highs and the lowest of the lows, resulting from enormous societal changes and disastrous decisions made in the aftermath of World War I that laid the groundwork for extraordinary global instability, the Great Depression, and the carnage that was unleashed in World War II.

Ben Graham was another person who invested during those times, and he was obviously greatly influential on Warren Buffett. I also loved the fact that he was fluent in Latin and Greek and was passionate about the classics. He was known to cite in Latin famous verses from books like the *Aeneid* while working or cleaning—not a routine I can claim to have adopted myself!

Taking the Road Less Traveled

I was married in 1989 at age twenty-three. I have a great wife (much more about her later) and two grown children, a boy and a girl. My daughter is a bit of an old soul. She shares a lot of the same musical interests that I do. One night, she showed me a blog entry written by a teenager who absolutely loved Joni Mitchell as we did. As my daughter read the blog out loud to me, we learned that Joni Mitchell had polio when growing up, which impaired her fingers in such a way that it made it impossible for her to create normal chord formations on a guitar. As a result, she had to make up her own chords as well as her own tuning, in such a way that it's almost impossible to replicate her songs. Mitchell apparently also began writing songs and poetry after she gave her daughter up for adoption. It was her way of speaking to her daughter.

That story truly exemplifies the power of taking the road less traveled. It also reminds me of what Bill Graham once said about the Grateful Dead: "They're not the best at what they do. They're the only ones that do what they do." To me, it's the flaws and the unique experiences that make people so interesting. I'm comfortable with working to have a picture unfold through effort and discovery versus having it painted for me. If it's painted for me, then it's painted for everybody else, and there is very little to be gained in those situations.

The point for me is that artists (who do the creating rather than simply admiring the end result) have an independent point of view from which they can find ultimate truths at a deeper level. That's why I often find myself gravitating to non–real estate people when I'm at events. I try to learn about their lives and what makes them tick, based on their own formative experiences. I have also seen similar characteristics among great investors as well, as they are able to make connections that others are unable to form and have the courage and resources to take action in order to prosper from the reality they see unfolding ahead of the crowd.

*   *   *

Joseph Campbell, one of the brilliant minds I have turned to for inspiration in my life, talked in his lectures about the Knights of the Round Table, and how when they went off on a quest it was not a group quest to achieve a specific goal. Rather, each individual knight entered the forest at a point of his choosing—usually at the darkest spot and where there was no clear path forward. The point of those Arthurian tales is that the treasure is buried deep in the darkest places of your psyche, and only you can go after it. No one else can tell you how to get there or what to go for.

I look in a similar way at my life and the decisions I've made during my journey: everything from deciding to go to college at UCLA to marrying my wife to becoming a Chartered Financial Analyst when everyone else in the real estate world tends to gravitate toward getting an MBA (which I also obtained). I also look back at the decision we made as a family to move up to Los Angeles when my son went to college so that my daughter could go to a specific private girls' school—a decision that changed our lives dramatically. Today, we're much more integrated in the

LA community, which is filled with artists and entertainment people. But it's 180 degrees different than Orange County, where we kept our principal home. Orange County is more business minded and much more conservative. But I've come to appreciate that; it has enabled me to venture forth to be challenged and to grow and evolve. Getting out of my comfort zone has allowed me to gain a diversity of experience.

In fact, I love to go to new cities without any plans: to just discover, walk, observe, and sense, finding patterns and the ways of being of the locals. Like Joni Mitchell, I like to form my own unique chords with my own customized tuning, using very special poetic words that produce incredibly timeless, beautiful music. At the end of the day, taking the road less traveled has allowed me to step back and see how madness can unfold in a way that allows me to alter my course and avoid the avalanche—or get back on the mountain when so few others will.

Learning to Separate the Signal from the Noise

Another key lesson I've come to appreciate as an investor is that it's really important to be independent and to separate the signal from the noise: to not let the crowd drown me out and have my reactions so heavily influenced by what others think or the pressure that's being put on me. And it's really materializing today in my consistent adherence to being a variable-rate borrower (as opposed to borrowing on a fixed rate; more on this later) in a world that appears to have a lot of fear about future inflation, interest rates rising materially, and deficits. My personal chess game has involved learning about how the monetary system works—and then transforming those insights into wealth-creating opportunities in a very unconventional way. This results from having a level of confidence and courage to do things that are completely counter to what most people think we should be doing.

I remember reading an interview in a magazine about Robert Plant of Led Zeppelin. In the article, the interviewer asked him why he was living in Austin, Texas.

He replied: "I'm just looking for clues; just trying to discover where I should be going next." I love that answer, because I relate to it closely. I don't know where my next "Aha!" moments are going to come from. But the multidisciplinary approach I developed through my liberal arts background, which includes my voracious appetite for reading and my inquisitive nature, allows me to perhaps have a wider antenna than others might possess or utilize.

However, this also can lead to a lot of noise to sift through—which is why it's so important for me to home in on where the signals truly are. Schopenhauer said that as we're going through life and we're making these individual decisions, they often seem like they're being done in a vacuum with no sense of guiding principle or pattern. But it's only when we look back on our lives that we realize that there truly was something more powerful guiding us. And whatever that force or intuition was, it's really up to us to figure it out.

I think a key goal in life is figuring out what your own personal unifying principle is. For me, it's been this desire to think about things a little differently so that I can generate insights that can make monumentally positive changes in my life and our investors' lives through wealth creation.

Chapter Three

THE POWER OF PARTNERSHIP

But it is still worse to take a decision without consulting a friend.
For a man may have the most excellent judgment in all other
matters, and yet go wrong in those which concern himself . . .
Therefore let a man take counsel of a friend. A doctor can cure
everyone but himself; if he falls ill, he sends for a colleague.
—Arthur Schopenhauer

For those who remember learning about the elements of the periodic table, you may recall the term "isotope." An isotope is a version of an element with the same number of protons but a different number of neutrons; uranium-232 and uranium-238 are examples. The presence of one additional (or one less) neutron inside the nucleus can greatly influence the stability and longevity of an element. For example, there is one element that has a half-life (the time it takes to decay by half) of four billion years, but its isotope (with one extra neutron) has a half-life of just one billionth of a second! While this is an extreme example, it is a great metaphor for all organizations, whether they are families, teams, governments, or businesses. The heart, soul, and stability of any organization is the nucleus: the parents, coaches, team leaders, civic leaders, political leaders, corporate leaders, and so on. Change one of them, and the effect may be bigger than we imagine.

While it's almost always dangerous to apply scientific principles rigidly to arenas dominated by human behavior—in this case, business—some powerful metaphors can be used to help us think differently about business, investing, and even life in general. So stay with me on this.

A nucleus is made up of protons and neutrons, and I will not even begin to attempt to address the subatomic world of the particle physics that describes the true (even smaller) building blocks of nature. The nucleus is so small relative to the size of an atom that it's equivalent to a penny on a football field. It is surrounded by electrons racing around in orbit around it. Despite its small size, the nucleus holds almost all of the mass of an atom. As shown above, depending upon the interaction of the nuclear particles, the nucleus can either be a source of great stability and longevity or the exact opposite. It is this recognition that I believe has helped CWS survive and prosper since 1969. We have always had a great nucleus, with the core particles working so well together.

Success in business is not a God-given right, particularly for the four-and-a-half decades CWS has been in business. At the heart of CWS is a partnership that has been critical to our success as we have watched so many others fall by the wayside. The company was founded as a partnership between Bill Williams and Jim Clayton, and it expanded with the fortuitous addition of Steve Sherwood in 1976. After Jim Clayton's retirement and Bill's desire to slow down, Steve never thought twice about continuing the partnership model. For him it allowed CWS to have the greatest chance of success. As such, I have been a partner for approximately twenty years, and one additional individual, Mike Engels, has been brought into the nucleus as well. I will write more about Mike a little later.

Being a fiduciary for other people's money is an enormous responsibility and honor, and it plays a hugely vital function in our free market economy. Collaboration is in our DNA at CWS, and it shapes how we view our relationships with investors. We view our investor relationships as another vital partnership that is critical to our success and longevity. With this partnership philosophy in mind, let's take a behind-the-scenes look at CWS. While I write extensively in this book about our investment ideas, philosophies, and the key trends influencing our capital deployment strategy, I have focused far less on communicating how we actually run our business. So I believe it is time for you to know more about the nucleus.

It Started with a Book

The first link in the CWS chain was the book *How I Turned $1,000 into a Million in Real Estate in My Spare Time* by William Nickerson. Within its pages, it describes how Nickerson was able to acquire, manage, and handle problems and opportunities in apartments. It turns out that two young fathers, Bill Williams and Jim Clayton, had both read the book, something they discovered one day during a conversation at their local YMCA at their kids' Indian Guides tribe meeting. At one point, Bill asked Jim: "Well, do you want to buy an apartment someday?" And Jim replied, "Yeah, sure."

Whether or not it seemed like a real plan at the time, Bill eventually found an apartment in Huntington Beach not far from where he lived. When he went to initially scout out the property, he asked his mother-in-law to go with him, because she had been in real estate for many years in North Carolina. As the story goes, she looked at it and said, "Yep, that's good."

The rub for Bill and Jim, though, was that in his book Nickerson said you should never buy a property for more than six times the gross annual income, and this particular building's asking price was set at seven times the gross. Reluctant to break from Nickerson's proven formula, Bill and Jim checked out the rents for similar apartments nearby. They turned out to be slightly higher. Bill wanted more information, so he knocked on the door of one of the competitive apartments and asked the resident, "Can I measure your apartment? I know this is abrupt, and I'll give you five dollars just for your time." She allowed him in, he measured it, and then he went back to the apartments that he and Jim were trying to buy and measured those; they were about the same size. That's when they realized that if they could raise their rent to match the other apartments, the price would equalize at six times gross. After talking it over, they agreed to take the chance and buy the property.

To do that, they needed to put $15,000 down on the $122,000 total purchase price—$7,500 each—which was equivalent to about half of each partner's life savings at that point. They went ahead and hired a manager and gave her a free apartment and a little bit of money. But they also had some lessons to learn in terms of managing their property, such as avoiding always going with the lowest bidder instead of working with reputable contractors.

They learned the hard way. They once hired some painters and agreed to the contract they proposed. A couple of hours later they drove back to the building to see how things were progressing—this was on a Saturday—and they were gone. Bill called them up and said, "Where are you guys?"

They said, "We are not going to do it."

Bill said, "What do you mean? We have a contract."

They said, "We don't care. We can't do it for the money that we agreed to, so we are not going to do it. Sue us."

In the end, Bill and Jim wound up doing all the painting themselves that day.

In the end, though, the purchase turned out to be a great investment; the pair doubled their initial investment in just a few years.

Steve Joins the Team

Fortune smiled on what was soon to become the team of CWS when, in 1976, Bill met Steve through their wives, who worked in the same department at Huntington Beach High School. When Bill learned that Steve was a sales engineer and had bought some condos in Phoenix, he offered him a job working with himself and Jim. But Steve, who had a nice, salaried job at the time, resisted.

Bill persisted, eventually offering Steve a situation where he would go out and find properties and become the third general partner in whatever he found. For Steve, who had read Napoleon Hill's classic book *Think and Grow Rich*, it was the tipping point for him to leave his corporate job and become an entrepreneur.

The first property he zeroed in on was in Phoenix: a community called Purple Sage. While they put it under contract, they didn't end up buying it. Instead, they decided to flip it and advertised it for sale. They eventually sold the option on the property to an investor from Santa Barbara who agreed to buy the property for $75,000 more than the contract price CWS had agreed to. That $75,000 became their seed capital.

The Big Breakthrough

The fortunes of the CWS team really turned, however, when Steve traveled to Texas in 1979 to scout out a portfolio of five mobile home parks owned by legendary real estate developer Trammell Crow. One of the properties, Stonegate Lewisville, cost $1.1 million—which the partners didn't have access to at the time. They each had about $35,000, which, cobbled together, was enough for a 10 percent down payment, but they needed to raise the rest of the capital from investors. It turned out to be a wise decision.

Stonegate Lewisville became a once-in-a-lifetime investment for CWS because, about three years after they bought the property, they received a call from another investor offering them $4 million for it. That certainly got their attention—until another called shortly after and offered them $5 million.

They knew $5 million was too much; it didn't make sense for a mobile home park buyer. Still, they couldn't figure out why the offers were coming in so high. So Steve traveled back to Texas to talk to brokers in the area to find out what was happening. After some back-and-forth with the broker, Steve finally got him to admit who the real buyer was: a shopping center developer that had tapped into savings and loan money.

With the broker out of the way, CWS got down to some real negotiations and eventually agreed to sell the property for $11 million—which generated an eighty-to-one return on the partners' original equity investment.

Growing the Partnership

Using that breakthrough as a foundation, Bill, Jim, and Steve built up CWS, not just through their financial savvy, but also by strengthening their partnership—which became a catalytic force for the company's growth in subsequent years. They set up annual planning sessions and talked through their individual goals for their lives and for the business. They would also conduct visualization exercises where they would contemplate questions such as how much time off a year they each wanted (the answer turned out to be five weeks).

They also never stopped trying to learn, which sometimes meant calling up companies much larger than they were and asking for help and advice on how they could continue to grow their business.

One of the key lessons they embraced early on was that the best way to do business—and especially with the bad times—is to keep communicating with your investors. In fact, the partners really went out of their way to be friends with their investors: playing tennis with them, sharing dinners, and the like. In the case of CWS, business was very personal.

They also held true to their values by agreeing that if they couldn't win the game fair and square, then it wasn't worth playing. That also meant they needed to remain realistic and optimistic at the same time—two forces that can sometimes be at odds with each other. But there was always an agreement to keep growing—to "keep the pedal to the metal as much as we could," as Bill put it—even during the more challenging years.

The partners also learned to leverage their different strengths. While Bill was more visionary, Steve was more practical and entrepreneurial: a great combination for filtering down the opportunities that were both aggressive and practical. "It was a good relationship that way," says Bill. "We both appreciated each other's doing that kind of thing. I think that when it got to the roughest and toughest points, we always said, 'Well, we have to do what's right here, for us and for our investors, and face it easily.' We were always willing to do that."

Another factor that came into play was that Steve was seventeen years younger than Bill, which brought balance in terms of how conservatively or aggressively they wanted the firm to grow. Similarly, I am seventeen years younger than Steve, which again has helped the firm balance the taste for growth that typically belongs to the young with the pragmatic experience we earn with age. I would offer the challenge that there are few, if any, other real estate firms that began in the 1960s that are still around today and thriving the way CWS is. It's amazing to consider that 99 percent of the investments we have made as a firm have been profitable. That's a testament to the fact that Bill and Steve respected the notion that they would never bet the farm or get caught up in buying properties for the wrong reasons.

For example, many firms were chasing properties to take advantage of changes in the tax law that went into effect in 1981, only to see these laws reversed in 1986, a development that helped bring down the S&Ls. A key lesson I've learned from Bill and Steve is that it is better to be generally right than precisely wrong when it comes to evaluating the potential of a new property. You can't grow a company with your foot on the brake the entire time, nor can you grow with balance if you never let up on the accelerator.

Another vital lesson the partners came to learn was that a key to success in the real estate business is to be patient. This meant not doing deals in some years even when investors were ready to hand over their capital. Because the partners valued their investors for more than their money, they waited until they were confident they had found a great opportunity. They also avoided those that were so big that they could sink the whole CWS ship if they were wrong. Bill and Steve came to call that principle "staying power," which meant that they would always run the firm in such a way that even during the toughest times they would have enough reserves to ride out the rough weather—something we all would experience soon enough as a team. But that was the key to making the business not just a business, but a *personal* business. When things did get bad and the business needed to ask its investors to put in more money in order to stay afloat, they had a strong relationship to work from. That's what the power of partnership is all about.

Chapter Four

THE GREAT EXCHANGE

Life is one big transition.
—Willie Stargell

The transition from mobile home parks was probably the most monumental strategic move we have made at CWS during our more than forty-five-year history. We looked at the environment, the changing fundamentals, and the very heated demand for large, but rare, manufactured housing community portfolios with seasoned management teams among newly formed real estate investment trusts (REITs) and some large institutional investors, and knew we had something that was highly desirable. Not as desirable as the Los Angeles Clippers were to Steve Ballmer (who broke all kinds of records when he bought the team for $2 billion), but still in demand. We also felt reasonably comfortable about making such a dramatic move, because we felt good about the landing spot for our capital: apartments, which we had been investing in for nearly ten years.

It was hard to grow in the manufactured housing business, since it was requiring deeper, more institutional capital—as opposed to our individual investor money—to go where the opportunities appeared to be: buying partially filled communities and developing new ones to accommodate the larger homes being purchased by home buyers. This required patient capital that didn't need an immediate return on investment and deep enough pockets to carry the investments until they passed the break-even point. In addition, the values being offered were compelling relative to a future we didn't find as rosy as the buyers seemed to believe.

On the other hand, we saw great, long-term opportunities to generate solid, risk-adjusted returns in apartments with much greater potential to scale the business. Rather than recount what I thought we were thinking and the reasons why we recommended making such a radical move with our investors, I thought it might be more interesting if I reprinted much of what we wrote to them in October 1997 as we were in the midst of heated negotiations with a few large potential acquirers and were seeking approval for the sale of the individual properties.

As you will see in the letter, deferring taxes from the sale of real estate via 1031 exchanges can be hugely beneficial to investors because of the additional return generated by investing with pre-tax dollars versus after-tax dollars. We have done more than $1 billion in 1031 exchanges for our investors since 1985, resulting in tremendous financial benefits. In fact, here is an example of a $45,000 investment made in 1985 into two mobile home parks and what has transpired since:

	1985	1985–April 2014	Multiple
Original Investment	$45,000		
Cash Distributed (through April 2014)		$131,164	2.91
Est. Value of Three Properties Now Invested in		$229,233	5.09
Totals	$45,000	$360,397	8.00

One can see the tremendous benefits of investing one's capital in income-producing properties and being able to reinvest the sale proceeds on a tax-deferred basis into new real estate investments. The two original investments are now invested in three apartment communities and have already returned a multiple of the original investment via previous cash distributions, much of which was sheltered from immediate taxation. In addition, the estimated value of the three investments is now approximately five times the original investment made back in 1985. This analysis does not take into account what would have happened had the distributions been reinvested.

All this helps to illustrate how valuable 1031 exchanges can be for real estate investors. Had this investor had to pay taxes after each sale, then he would have had far less capital working for him, which would have translated into lower dividends and less value today.

We endeavor to carry out 1031 exchanges for virtually every property sale. With this background, the following information about the large portfolio transaction takes on more relevance, since we communicated our intentions to reinvest the sale proceeds via tax-deferred 1031 exchanges and the projected benefits for doing so.

We structured the sale of approximately twenty-five properties (and our management company) in a $225 million transaction as a series of put options that had to be exercised within twenty-four months and with at least thirty days' notice. This was done to allow us to carry out an orderly reinvestment of the more than $100 million in capital without being under great pressure to buy properties at inflated prices, since there are some very precise time constraints that must be adhered to in order to qualify for a 1031 tax-deferred exchange.

Once a sale is consummated, the exchanger has forty-five days to nominate (typically) up to three properties in which to reinvest the proceeds and six months from the date of sale to complete the purchase.

We could not have lined up enough quality properties at fair prices in that short a period of time. For this reason we gave ourselves two years in which to reinvest the money, and when we found properties to buy, we notified the purchaser within thirty days which ones we wanted to sell. It was quite a brilliantly designed transaction, if I must say so myself.

It allowed us to have tremendous buying power despite being relatively small players in the apartment industry, enabled us to purchase some great properties, and permitted us to invest in the infrastructure ahead of the growth, since we were assured of its taking place. It also allowed us to create some scale and a much stronger industry reputation to attract talent and be in good standing with the brokerage community. As serious players, we had the opportunity to compete for the properties that we thought offered the most compelling value.

It is interesting that in the letter (which appears in the following section), we didn't point to the euphoric conditions taking place in the industry with the huge amount of Wall Street money hungrily seeking loans originated to mobile home borrowers so they could be packaged and sold off to investors in different tranches. We viewed this as an accident waiting to happen. We definitely discussed it internally, but we preferred to focus on the euphoric interest in what we had to sell with regard to our investor communications. We wanted to avoid creating fear if the sale did not go through. Nevertheless, our intuition and timing turned out to be spot on. In fact, the Creekside property mentioned earlier was available for sale approximately ten years later, and we would not have paid $10 million for it, even after having sold it for $21 million. Demand conditions had deteriorated so dramatically due to the implosion of the lending business for manufactured home buyers, and at the same time, single-family homes became much more accessible due to their supply and easy credit. Okay, now it's time for the letter.

Our Letter to Investors

We sent the following letter to our investors:

> On October 6 and 7, 1997, special meetings were held to present potential sale opportunities for many of our manufactured housing partnerships. A number of years ago we

presented a plan to suspend distributions from some of our properties in order to make the necessary investments in marketing and infrastructure to prepare our communities for better times that inevitably lay ahead. During this time we were also well aware that the real estate investment trust (REIT) revolution was in its embryonic stage. It was becoming clear that an extraordinary amount of capital was being formed to purchase real estate on behalf of publicly traded companies. More importantly, this trend was beginning to present itself for the first time in the manufactured housing industry as three companies went public in 1993 and 1994.

During this time we determined that it was a good time to sell our communities in a package because we believed we could obtain a *premium price*. We emphasize premium because we were confident that the economy was going to improve and our properties were positioned to increase in value. We entered into contract with two of the REITs only to see them attempt to lower the price at the end. This was unacceptable to us and we decided to hold the communities knowing that this was a very good option as well. As most of us have experienced a substantial increase in dividends, we're happy we held firm on our price.

Despite the good times, we are still aware that many of our properties are approaching twenty-five years of age or older. We have always felt that we couldn't hold these assets forever. Fortunately, we have come to another great point in the historical evolution of the manufactured housing industry. As Yogi Berra said, "It's déjà vu all over again." Interest rates are low, REITs have performed well and created enormous investor confidence, and there are very few large portfolios of manufactured home communities remaining. In addition, one new phenomenon has been added to the mix. Namely, large institutions see tremendous value in purchasing existing companies with experienced management teams and industry knowledge to build a world-class real estate organization. CWS happens to have this, particularly in the manufactured housing industry.

Given the confluence of all these factors, we believe that this represents a great time to sell our communities because extraordinary premiums are being paid for large portfolios of well-managed manufactured home communities. These premiums are being paid by both REITs and institutional investors seeking to get into the industry. In our opinion, the worst thing we can do now is to do nothing. To quote Yogi Berra one last time, "When you come to a fork in the road, take it." Our properties are well positioned and the prices are fantastic. Our job is to pick the right horse and ride it to the finish line.

Sale Process

Given our somewhat negative experience with two of the existing REITs, we are inclined to favor entering into a letter of agreement with the institutional investor. To reiterate, our two most important criteria are to pick the purchaser with the highest probability of closing at our target price and the one who will be most accommodating in our need to carry out 1031 exchanges for the selling partnerships.

Because the institutional investor is aggressively seeking to enter the manufactured housing industry, we currently have more confidence in its ability to close at a price closest to our target and to be most flexible in staging the sales over a two-year period to accommodate our need for 1031 exchanges. We anticipate this long sale process for two reasons: (1) some of the properties are currently increasing their occupancy through filling vacant spaces and the highest value will be achieved if they are sold in 1999 when they have reached stabilized occupancy, and (2) upon selling each property we only have forty-five days to nominate three exchange candidates. This is a very short time frame. Rather than being pressured to find a property, we would rather identify the reinvestment candidate first and then trigger the sale in order to ensure we are making the best investment decisions.

Despite our belief that the institutional investor is the optimal candidate, we will remain true to our target prices because we believe that the REITs have probably learned from their mistakes. They are well aware that we will not back down from our price once the properties are under contract. As a result, they most likely will be a little more diligent in determining the prices for our properties before putting them under contract. The fact also remains that we still have one of the few remaining large portfolios and there is no reason to price this highly sought-after asset modestly.

Tax Impact from Sale

In our opinion, the third chart is the most significant. It identifies the tax impact of the sale and compares the cash flow generated at 8 percent for an investor who exchanges versus one who invests with after-tax dollars. (Please note that the tax impact for the partnership may be different than what appears on your individual schedules because these represent partnership averages.) These two numbers are then compared to the current cash flow being distributed from the properties. The results overwhelmingly show the benefits of reinvesting with tax-deferred dollars. Obviously in every case the cash flow generated by reinvesting pre-tax dollars is significantly greater than when after-tax proceeds are used. What is surprising, however, is how much greater the cash flow would be by selling the manufactured housing communities and reinvesting the proceeds tax-deferred in new investments generating 8 percent returns on the sale proceeds. The following portfolio summary should bring this to light:

	Low Scenario	High Scenario
Current Cash Flow	2,410,396	2,410,396
Cash Flow at 8% after 1031 Exchange	4,339,650	4,885,440
Cash Flow at 8% Investing After-Tax $ (No Exchange)	2,094,675	2,467,661
1031 Exchange Cash Flow versus Current Cash Flow	+80%	+103%
1031 Exchange Cash Flow versus After-Tax Cash Flow	+107%	+98%

In our opinion, the table above is striking in its conclusions. We project to increase distributions on capital that is reinvested tax-deferred at 8 percent by between 80 and 103 percent as compared to what is being produced today by the manufactured housing portfolio. In addition, because many of the properties being sold are older and have minimal depreciable basis and relatively low debt, they are producing a fair amount of taxable income. By carrying out a 1031 exchange, however, we are able to buy a larger property using borrowed funds. This results in more of our cash flow being sheltered from tax because we have a higher depreciable basis. Thus, not only do we project higher cash distributions, but a greater percentage of it being sheltered from taxes.

It was a beautifully designed and executed plan except for one thing: our timing was terrible in terms of when we bought the apartments and how they were financed. This is the subject of the next chapter.

Chapter Five

CATACLYSMIC INTERFACE

*To overcome difficulties is to experience the full delight of
existence, no matter where the obstacles are encountered; whether
in the affairs of life, in commerce or business; or in mental
effort—the spirit of inquiry that tries to master its subject. There
is always something pleasurable in the struggle and the victory.*
—Arthur Schopenhauer

I've titled this chapter "Cataclysmic Interface" because of a conversation I had with a business associate of Steve Sherwood's. I was lamenting to him my fear and consternation about having to convey some bad news to a group of investors, and he knowingly shook his head and said, "Ah, the cataclysmic interface." That expression was so perfect to describe how I was viewing the situation. It is extremely cathartic to deal directly with challenges, and to communicate openly and honestly with investors so as to enroll them in the solution. A good description of this is from a lesson conveyed in Yogananda's *Autobiography of a Yogi*:

> My mother once tried to frighten me with an appalling story
> of a ghost in a dark chamber. I went there immediately, and

expressed my disappointment at having missed the ghost. Mother never told me another horror-tale. Moral: Look fear in the face and it will cease to trouble you.

Background to the Cataclysmic Interface

One of the most important lessons we learned from the late 1990s and the year 2000 was that we didn't give our debt strategy much thought. We were caught in "rearview mirror investing," fearful that what turned out to be an extraordinarily rare event in financial history, the crippling high interest rates of the late 1970s and early 1980s, would repeat itself. Consequently, we thought we would be crazy not to lock in long-term, fixed-rate financing for our properties, especially since interest rates had been coming down to a level such that we could now borrow for ten years at 8 percent. That actually seemed somewhat reasonable in 1999 and 2000, given how robust the economy was—considering the dot-com boom, the healthy housing market, and the resulting strong job growth. So the question one had to answer was, could these good times last? There was always that fear that interest rates would go a lot higher, as they had in the early 1980s. But as Plato said, "Courage is knowing what not to fear."

We made a mistake when we discussed our debt decisions. We used to say that we don't get paid to predict interest rates; how wrong we were. The reason we were wrong is because we were finding ourselves locked into loans that would be extremely expensive to prepay in the event we wanted to either refinance properties or sell them and not have the buyer assume the loans. These loans had yield maintenance penalties when taken out on a fixed-rate basis. It was very typical that for all but three to six months of the loan term, the lender wanted to be compensated for getting its money back early. The yield maintenance formula assumed that the lender was able to get that money back and reinvest it essentially at the rate of interest he was already getting, less the corresponding treasury yield of a similar maturity to the loan's due date.

For example: If the loan had an interest rate of 8 percent and we wanted to prepay the loan with seven years remaining, then the formula would subtract the difference between this and the Treasury yield (let's say 4.50 percent) to give an annual loss of yield of (in this example) 3.50 percent. This figure would then be multiplied by seven (the number of years remaining on the loan) and then reduced somewhat to account for getting one's money back today versus seven years from now. Cutting to the chase, this would equate to approximately 15 to 20 percent of the loan amount as a penalty. It was extremely expensive and almost always not worth the price.

The high prepayment penalty tremendously harmed the marketability of the property, because any buyer would be forced to assume a loan that had an interest rate higher than the current market rate (and oftentimes with lower leverage than would be desirable). This would lower the value of the property quite significantly compared with properties being marketed to buyers able to place their own debt. In addition, having such high prepayment penalty debt eliminated property owners from refinancing their loans in the event interest rates dropped.

When the Shoes Started to Drop

We learned this firsthand as rates dropped, because the economy went into a terrible recession with the dot-com implosion and resulting job losses. The corresponding drop in occupancy among apartment communities such as ours resulted from many young workers being the first ones to be laid off. Those who had stable jobs were incentivized to go buy homes as rates started to drop significantly. What follows is a specific example of a challenging situation we faced:

In 2002 and 2003 we were contending with significant drops in revenue; with the inability to refinance our debt, we would have to bring new capital to the table. This was a particularly challenging situation, because the loan in question had many years left on it. Supporting this investment required a leap of faith on the part of the investors, because no one wants to toss funds into a black hole. However, we did end up recapitalizing it.

Whenever we have brought in new capital it has turned out to be a wise decision, because the property has tended to turn around and the money is then returned with interest. The additional money earns a competitive rate of return and allows the investors to bridge the gap until the original capital is returned, typically with a profit. In this case, it was no different, but I won't tell you how this story ends just yet.

The case of the Marquis at Town Centre in Broomfield, Colorado, illustrates this point well. We bought this property in 2000 and put a ten-year, 8 percent fixed-rate loan on it to help finance the purchase. Denver was decimated by the tech downturn, having tremendous exposure to telecom jobs that were eviscerated after the tech bubble burst and venture capital and IPO money dried up. During the darkest of times, it is often hard to see a much brighter future ahead. Most of us have a tendency to extrapolate current conditions into the future rather than being able to envision something very different.

We were faced with the need to raise additional capital to support the investment. We knew in the long run we would be okay, because we had a great property at a terrific location in a city with a very favorable long-term future. We were also confident that even though it was going to take another seven years to get out of the debt, interest rates would be a lot less than 8 percent. The following table shows the precarious situation we found ourselves in during 2003.

	Projected in 2003
Revenue	2,873,000
Expenses	(1,293,000)
Net Operating Income	1,580,000
Capital Expenditures	(127,000)
Cash Flow Before Debt Service	1,453,000
Debt Service	(2,159,000)
Cash Flow	(706,000)

To say we were in a precarious position is an understatement. And Town Centre was not the only property we had facing a similar set of circumstances. We were fighting multiple financial fires at properties suffering from declining revenues and high-cost, fixed-rate loans that could not be prepaid for a number of years. This prevented us from taking advantage of the lower interest rates that were available due to the Greenspan Fed's dramatic reduction in the federal funds rate (which spilled over to the cost of apartment loans dropping significantly). We had no choice but to go to our investors and ask them to invest more capital until we could refinance and dramatically lower our fixed costs.

We do everything possible to prevent losing properties to our lenders, because we learned during our manufactured housing days that financial and emotional staying power are almost always rewarded in the long run once the shakeout of weak players and lenders has taken place, new supply is curtailed due to poor loan performance, and operations have improved as the economy heals and demand outpaces supply. As previously mentioned, every time we brought in capital to support our investments, all of the new money was returned plus generating a minimum annual return of 8 percent, and the original equity investment was returned plus a profit. Perhaps in some cases we would have been smarter to cut the cord and spend our time and money on more productive ventures than saving a property that was in distress, yet giving up was not and is not in our DNA. We have a fierce tenacity when the chips are down, and failure is not an option. That is not to say that fighting these fires did not take a personal toll on me. The stress was ever present and there were many sleepless nights.

We made a big bet on an industry (apartments) that was decimated by policy measures taken by the Federal Reserve and the Bush administration. These measures were designed to keep the economy afloat by stimulating massive appreciation in housing values through a dramatic reduction in the cost and accessibility of mortgage capital. Our customers—high-income, white-collar knowledge workers—were either laid off at a historically unprecedented rate, or they bought homes just when our markets were constructing a large quantity of new apartments in the face of dwindling demand. This, combined with our suboptimal financing decisions, not only cost our investors and CWS dearly, but also rocked me to my core and forced a certain amount of unexpected soul-searching upon me about what it takes to be successful in business. Although I strongly believed that things were getting better and would be much improved in a few years, it didn't lessen the pain of producing deeply disappointing results for those properties purchased prior to 2002.

What Really Matters

The one thing that motivates me more than anything in my job is to make a difference in the lives of our investors, employees, and residents. Few things are as fulfilling to me as hearing about how our investors could retire early, send their kids to a private college, purchase their dream home, take a never previously contemplated vacation, or fund a favorite charity—partially or entirely because of the success of their CWS investments. When I hear stories about this I say to myself that all of the travel, family separation, hard work, and challenges are worth it. This is why I come to work every day.

Given this personal insight, one can then see that producing poor results is something I take very personally, no matter how powerful some of the environmental forces were. This experience has reinforced in me

George Soros's belief that no one has a monopoly on the truth and that human beings are fallible and should always be questioning their actions, motivations, and decision-making processes. After all, as previously mentioned, we can never divorce the observer from the observed, because the mere act of observing something can change what is being observed.

I am humble, flawed, and constantly at risk of making serious errors influenced by optimism, pessimism, or whatever else is impacting how I see the world. You must know that anyone to whom you entrust your money is subjected to the same human shortcomings as yourself. But what I can say is that CWS is an organization of extraordinary integrity, humanity, openness, and skill, and has a hunger to not only survive but also prosper over the long term. We do not hide bad news from our investors—remember the Cataclysmic Interface—and we make every effort to keep our investors fully informed at all times. We are partners, we honor our relationships, and we would expect nothing less in return.

I was truly sorry for disappointing our investors. The world changed in ways we never anticipated, but perhaps we should have. At the same time, they were incredibly supportive and trusting in us, backing us despite their frustration and disappointment. After all, we weren't the only ones whose financial results were less than projected. The NASDAQ had dropped by nearly 80 percent from peak to trough, so the economy was definitely facing a lot of challenges.

One of the key lessons I learned was that we *are* in the business of predicting interest rates and key economic trends. When we borrow 75–80 percent of the value of a property with the potential to lock in loans that cannot be economically prepaid if interest rates drop, then we are in the interest-rate forecasting business, whether we like it or not. For this reason, I now spend an extraordinary amount of time contemplating the major economic forces that can influence interest rates and job growth so that we can make better capital allocation decisions. Spoiler alert: This will come into play as we embark upon our Munger Moment in the midst of the Great Recession.

Our debt strategy and overriding emphasis on using variable-rate loans to finance the acquisition of new properties and refinance existing assets in our portfolio was one of the most important strategic decisions we made, and it has paid enormous dividends so far. This bias toward variable-rate loans with low-cost prepayment penalties was a direct result of the trials and initiation we went through during the downturn from 2000–2003. The courage (knowing what not to fear) to use variable-rate financing came from an obsession on my part to study historical interest-rate trends and what interest rates and inflation did in the 1930s in the midst of the Great Depression.

Remember Town Center? Are you curious as to how it did? Let's fast-forward ten years and see what has happened since then to see if our optimism in 2003 was warranted. Here is how the property performed in 2014:

	2014	Change from 2003
Revenue	4,516,000	57.2%
Expenses	(1,493,000)	15.5%
Net Operating Income	3,023,000	91.3%
Capital Expenditures	(824,000)	648.8%
Cash Flow Before Debt Service	2,199,000	51.3%
Debt Service	(1,850,000)	
Cash Flow	349,000	$1.055 million

It was a remarkable turnaround. The combination of revenue growth dramatically exceeding the growth in expenses along with lower interest rates led to cash flow improving by nearly $1.1 million; the property is now cash-flow positive. We have been able to make significant investments in the property to keep it first rate. We were able to return all of the additional capital invested during the downturn, and the original investors are now getting regular distributions. We are also amortizing the loan so that each year we are paying down an amount equal to nearly 4 percent of one's original investment.

Chapter Six

THE STUDENT
BECOMES THE SPEAKER

Successful investing is anticipating the anticipation of others.
—*John Maynard Keynes*

My love of writing with the goal of communicating thoroughly and effectively eventually led me, starting in the late 1990s, to start writing quarterly and annual letters to our investors. I have since written hundreds of pages and given many presentations for our investors at our annual meetings and for specific investments for which we are raising money. Those writings and speeches reflected our thought processes in the moment and helped explain the hypotheses we were forming based on the information we had at hand. Taking on these tasks required me to make time to reflect and employ the discipline needed to pull together disparate sources of information as a way to get a better sense of the big picture the data was hinting at. Only then could I identify the right course to take for our firm.

As I mentioned before, it's easy to reconstruct events and thoughts with the benefit of hindsight, but this cannot be done for those who have to lay their point of view and predictions on the line in the moment, when the heat is turned up to its highest point. For this reason, some of what follows will be material that was written as events were unfolding via the letters I wrote to our investors. It may be modified to make it more readable and/or relevant. But the intention is for the reader to understand what I was thinking at the time.

Please remember that my goal has been to recognize and take advantage of those Munger Moments, which obviously need to be taken advantage of in real time. I feel inauthentic if I'm sharing retrospectively when I have so much "in the moment" material available—warts and all.

In working through all that research and analysis, I became intrigued with a very interesting creature: the investment bubble. A bubble is an event where investments become overvalued or overheated in some way—think of the dot-com or housing crazes for context—with the inevitable result that the bubble will eventually pop, usually with disastrous results. Well, it can be disastrous if you've bought into the euphoria. But bubbles can also present opportunities if you have the patience to wait until they've burst.

In my work, I began to obsess over identifying the conditions and characteristics that signaled a bubble was at hand. What follows are some of the important observations, predictions, and conclusions that we generated at CWS over the years to help prepare us for the 2005–2007 bubble and its aftermath.

The Rise of the Housing Bubble

In March 2005, I stated at our annual investor meeting that anyone buying a house in Orange County, California, should have a ten-year horizon and should be comfortable with losing paper wealth during that period of time: "Housing, especially in California, is dead money for many years to come. Game over!"

Virtually every investment boom/bubble has the same characteristics. The perception that easy money can be made with little risk is reinforced by the media and cocktail chatter, which serves to suck in the public (i.e., the "dumb money"). Those who believe they are very smart want to brag about how smart they are by saying how well their investments are doing, and those not in the game feel stupid and behind their neighbors on the path to the American Dream. Other characteristics of an investment mania are a lot of borrowing, fraud at the tail end of the boom, questionable-quality supply of whatever is in high demand, and then a crash.

Prior to the housing boom, the most recent financial bubble had been the dot-com/telecom craze of 1995–2000. Let's compare the dot-com/telecom bubble with the housing bubble:

	Dot Com/Telecom	Housing
Public participation	Enormous numbers of day traders.	Large numbers of condo flippers and investor/speculators.
A lot of borrowing	Huge margin debt and massive corporate spending on technology.	Enormous amount of mortgage lending, much of which is highly risky given the repayment terms and interest rate risk.
Fraud	Illegal IPO allocation, fraudulent accounting, and backdating of stock options. Just think of Enron and Worldcom.	Widespread appraisal fraud and false information provided on loan applications encouraged by shady mortgage brokers. Massive accounting irregularities by Fannie Mae and Freddie Mac.
Questionable supply	Junk companies going public, with most of them failing.	Massive numbers of condo conversions of basic apartments and a large amount of new condo construction.
Crash	NASDAQ dropped 80%	Housing prices falling rapidly in areas that experienced great appreciation, inventory exploding, and new home sales down by 25% from the peak.

With second-home purchasers and speculators no longer buying and in many cases selling, the supply and demand got out of whack. Inventory of new and existing homes for sale reached a record level, and it was taking longer and longer to sell homes. Since basic economic laws cannot be repealed, the only way to clear the market was by lowering prices, which the major builders were doing very aggressively, first by offering incentives like upgrades or subsidized interest rates, and then by slashing prices, particularly in high-cost areas like California, Florida, and the East Coast.

We had been here before, especially CWS with our extensive history in manufactured housing. We had had the lovely challenge of selling new homes in a soft market in which we were competing with lower-priced resales. As we had to move our prices lower, this obviously impacted those existing residents trying to sell their homes, and they were not happy. When people's equity and financial security are at risk, they begin to look for ways to recoup their losses and respond to their fears. The most common method is through litigation, and I predicted that we would see a rash of lawsuits against builders, particularly condo developers and apartment converters in communities that only sold a portion of the units and went back to renting the rest.

Another important firsthand lesson we learned in the manufactured housing industry had to do with the insidiousness of poor lending practices and outright fraud. There were many changes happening in the manufactured housing industry in the 1990s that caught our attention. These were so profound that we realized we had to make a strategic move to either exit the family park business (locations open to all ages as opposed to adult communities that are restricted to ages 55+) or significantly recapitalize our business so that we could better compete in what was going to be a difficult environment. Our intuition was correct in that the industry had gone through much upheaval in the previous eight years, and much of it was caused by easy money and poor lending practices.

In 1998, the year we entered into our agreement to sell our manufactured housing communities, shipments of manufactured housing hit a cycle high of 373,000 units. The lending spigot was turned on full blast; one year later new lending peaked at $13.5 billion. Just after this, the fraud and horrible lending practices became more visible as the defaults began to materialize. This scared Wall Street investors, who no longer wanted to buy manufactured housing loans without an enormous interest rate premium to home loans. Suddenly lending completely dried up, home prices collapsed, and transaction volume shrank considerably. Shipments dropped to 131,000 in 2004 and new loans went down to $500 million (from $13.5 billion) in 2005. Talk about a collapse! Yet this is what happens when lending becomes too accessible and unscrupulous characters enter the industry to make easy money by doling out easy money.

We have also experienced the benefits of entering a market when lending has contracted and asset values have collapsed as a result. This was the case when we first started buying apartments in 1988–1991 in Texas. As mentioned previously, the tax law changed in 1986, no longer allowing passive losses to be used to reduce ordinary income for non–real estate professionals. This devastated those sponsors whose business models were based on offering attractive tax shelters for high-income earners. When this was combined with the hugely corrupt savings and loan industry, commercial real estate (including apartments) was set up for a big fall. Capital exited the industry, since it was badly misallocated because of perverse incentives in the tax code and the lax regulatory environment for S&Ls.

New apartment lending was $33.5 billion in 1986, and by 1992 it was -$12.9 billion. Yes, that was a *negative* $12.9 billion, as loans were written off and thousands of properties were foreclosed. Commercial lending took an even more devastating trajectory as new loan originations peaked at $86 billion in 1988 and fell to -$43.6 billion in 1992. Both industries recovered sharply within thirteen years as net new lending to apartments reached $71.2 billion in 2005 and $254.8 billion for commercial loans in 2005 (this data is from the Federal Reserve).

Manufactured housing, commercial real estate, and apartments cannot compare in magnitude to the traditional home lending market in size and importance to the economy. Commercial and multifamily (primarily apartments) loans totaled $1.6 trillion in 2000, growing by $1.2 trillion in six years, while home loans grew by $4.7 trillion (to $9.8 trillion) during this same time frame. Within six years an exotic array of repayment and interest-rate options were created to make sure that every living and breathing individual could buy a home, whether they were financially and emotionally prepared or not. The message went something like this:

> You don't have a down payment? No problem. We'll either arrange for 100 percent financing or get a foundation to gift you a down payment because they think it is God's desire for you to own a home. Oh, don't worry about the fees they are making on the transaction or that their foundation is endowed with money gifted to it by homebuilders.

> You have credit card debt you need to pay off? No problem, we'll lend you 125 percent of the value of your home and consolidate all your debt. You're worried that you may not have enough income to qualify for the loan? No sweat; we'll fill out a "stated income" loan where the lender doesn't verify your income, just takes your word for it. You do make $75,000 per year, right?

At CWS we had been saying that there were millions of people who were renters who didn't really know it, because they technically owned a home—one that was 100 percent leveraged. From 1970 to 1981 the US homeownership rate was between 64.3 and 66 percent, while from 1982 to 1994 it was 63.5 to 64.4 percent. After 1995 it went from

64.2 percent to 69.2 percent, an enormous increase in market share for owner-occupied housing. Consequently, it devastated the apartment market, sucking a lot of people from renting into homeownership. There was also a dramatic increase in the vacancy rate of single-family homes. Between 1970 and 1994 the highest it reached was 4.9 percent; in the fourth quarter of 2005 it reached 10.2 percent (according to the Census Bureau) and dropped to 9.3 percent in the second quarter of 2006. This suggests that a large number of second-home buyers and investor/speculators purchased many of these homes. The bottom line is that too much supply had been created, and Wall Street agreed: homebuilders' stock prices fell by 40 to 60 percent from their peak, and new home sales dropped significantly.

My assertion is that all investment manias have the common characteristics of the perception of easy profits with little or no risk, loose lending standards, and outright fraud and deceit. This housing boom had been fueled by a mortgage finance bubble on an unprecedented scale that would have enormous economic implications as it unwound. I had been saying that long-term interest rates had very little risk of going much higher, because the economic carnage left behind from the housing market bubble deflating would be too much for the economy to bear.

I would like to share a little anecdote from TheHousingBubbleBlog.com, one of my favorite housing-related websites at the time. This is from an entry I read in 2006, when subprime lending was nearing its apex. While one never knows for sure if the posters of messages are legitimate, I felt this one was genuine, and thought I would share it because it was so informative and shocking with regard to how weak the borrowers had become, especially in high-cost areas like San Diego, where this individual worked. Here's the post (my comments are bracketed):

> I am quite new to real estate investing. It would seem that I know 1/10 about RE investing as many of the regular contributors to this board and even less than the "experts."

Sometimes, however, I think that the "experts" should just spend one week in my office observing the financial profiles of our refinance applicants. I believe their outlook would be much different.

Most people simply cannot believe the profiles that we see. I am the sales manager of a branch office of a top-10 national lender. My office of 7 loan officers takes +/- 100 loan applications per week, 90% of that coming from cold calls.

Of the last 100, I have taken some simple statistics and have found the following:

- 68/100 had LTV's [loan-to-value percentages] over 80% at time of application
- 16/100 had LTV's over 100% at time of application
- 78/100 had back end DTI's [debt-to-income ratio] over 55%
- 31/100 had back end DTI's over 70%
- 23/100 had FICO's [creditworthiness ratings] under 500
- 81/100 had credit card debt above $10,000
- 54/100 had credit card debt above $20,000
- 18/100 had credit card debt above $50,000
- 66/100 had Pay-option ARMs [adjustable-rate mortgages]
- 27/100 had Pay-option ARMs and mortgage lates [late payments on mortgage loans]
- 22/100 were either in forbearance or had been in forbearance within the past 12 months [these loans were in default, but the lenders were not pursuing collection or foreclosure proceedings at that time]

We took 14 applications today and we cannot qualify a single borrower for any type of loan. We are subprime, in fact, sometimes I say we are sub-subprime. We can qualify almost anyone for a loan. Not today.

Let me tell you about just one borrower from today:

- Husband and wife
- Husband on fixed income military retirement $1800/mo
- Wife makes $9500/mo as a registered nurse
- 5 properties with $3,400,000 in mortgages
- All mortgages currently have prepays
- 8 interest-only mortgages
- 1 option ARM deferring $3500/mo
- 3 in Chula Vista and 2 in Escondido
- No more than $75,000 equity in any of the homes (verified by comp checks with 3 appraisers)
- All properties with front end LTV over 90%
- $65,000 credit card debt
- $672 Mercedes payment
- One property had 3 mortgages, one of them hard money
- 621 mid FICO
- 2x30 in the past 12 months [two payments more than thirty days past due]
- Not a dime in the bank

They have been making mortgage payments with their credit cards and refinancing to pay off the credit cards. They are at the end of their rope, but refuse to throw in the towel.

This is not even an "extreme" example. I could show you dozens of these every single week. I just wish the experts would see what I see. I think the statistics released would be different. Granted, I only see applications from San Diego and Imperial Counties, but this is just getting out of hand.[1]

The couple referenced in this blog post had lost sight of the fact that the primary purpose of your home should be for shelter and enjoyment, not exclusively a source of wealth creation.

The Lola Economy and the Confirmation Bias

Investors—indeed, all humans—are psychologically biased. Yet the hindsight bias is but one of the many psychological biases that affect our judgment as investors.

I've found that a great way to illustrate that truth is by using the story of one of the world's greatest rock 'n' roll songwriters as my vehicle for documenting the psychological investing trap known as "the confirmation bias." The rock 'n' roll writer in question is the Kinks' front man Ray Davies, and the song is "Lola."

"Lola" is one of the classic songs in rock and roll. It has that distinctive opening riff, and the unmistakable voice of Ray Davies. It also has some amazing lyrics that not only tell a riveting story about a young lad encountering the big, bad world of London for the first time but also offers some pretty terrific lessons for investors. Of course, it takes a bit of a twisted mind to make that connection—but you have to play the hand that was dealt to you, so I'll just roll with it (to paraphrase another British rock 'n' roll band, Oasis).

The song ("Lola," not "Roll With It") is a great metaphor for the

---

1. Mike Shedlock, *The Housing Bubble Blog*, Comment on "Bits Bucket And Craigslist Finds For September 18, 2006," Sept. 18, 2006, http://thehousingbubbleblog.com/?p=1468, containing link to post from Smithosity on SDCIA Message Board, Sept. 9, 2006, http://sdcia.websitetoolbox.com /post?id=1382618.

extraordinary runaway train of our credit markets from 2002 to 2006, particularly in the area of residential mortgages. It is sung in the first person, and we are introduced to the narrator immediately as he recounts the encounter he had with a woman he met in London. They met in a club, where she approached him and asked him to dance, introducing herself as Lola.

So far so good: all pretty harmless stuff. It's safe to say that nothing out of the ordinary is going on, similar to the mortgage finance market that was functioning normally by qualifying borrowers based on verifiable income, legitimate down payments, and a strong credit history providing evidence of consistent repayment of obligations. In 2001 subprime loan originations totaled $120 billion and represented a little less than 5 percent of all new loans generated, and government-sponsored agencies like Fannie Mae and Freddie Mac represented about 50 percent of the lending in that year.

Back to the song. We hear how they danced together, and then he noticed something a little strange—but he didn't think much of it at the time. Lola squeezed him unusually hard, and she sure didn't walk like most women do.

Isaac Asimov said that the most exciting phrase to hear in science, the one that heralds new discoveries, is not "Eureka!" but "That's funny . . ." It's important that we pay attention to subtle cues that make us think a second time. Unfortunately neither our protagonist nor our lenders and regulators took a step back in reflection when some atypical things started occurring. I would characterize this as 2002, when subprime lending increased by 50 percent while total volume grew by 30 percent. Despite this very rapid growth, subprime originations still only represented about 6.4 percent of all new loans originated—far below the radar screen of most market observers. During this year we saw the introduction of interest-only subprime loans, but with only 1 percent of new loans being interest-only.

Things began to get a lot more interesting with Lola as she invited our protagonist to come home with her. Everything was perfect; he was falling for her. The world might be awry, but not Lola. She was there all for him. He didn't want the night to end.

I would describe this as the "honeymoon phase" of the relationship. Passion was heating up, they were getting to know each other better, they couldn't be apart, and our hero thought Lola was very special and unique. This takes us through 2003, when things started to get hot and heavy in the lending market. Interest rates dropped dramatically, everyone was looking to refinance, and subprime growth was continuing to outpace overall lending growth. New subprime loan originations grew from $185 billion to $310 billion (a 67.6 percent increase) between 2002 and 2003 while overall lending shot up from $2.885 trillion to $3.945 trillion (36.7 percent growth). That was an unprecedented period in the history of US residential mortgage financing. Subprime lending now represented 7.9 percent of all new loans originated, 6 percent of which were interest-only. Thirty percent of loans had a combined loan-to-value in excess of 90 percent, and approximately 33 percent of loans had minimal documentation. While in aggregate the trend of loosening credit standards was of some concern, in general, underwriting was still fairly solid and property values were continuing to escalate.

Things would begin to change much more significantly over the next few years, however—as would Lola. After only leaving home for the first time a week ago, he had now kissed a woman for the first time: a woman who declaratively stated that she was going to catalyze his transition to manhood.

This is when things started getting crazy. Our hero was overcome with desire. After all, he had just left home the previous week and had never experienced the kiss of a woman before, and suddenly he had the full attention of the beautiful Lola. He was now putty in her hands, willing to go anywhere and do anything she asked. I would say that this is 2004–2006 in the home lending market.

It was at this stage that people who were previously shut out of the mortgage market were taken in hand by lenders and mortgage brokers (with the encouragement of Wall Street) and were told, "We're going to make the American Dream come true for you." No money down, no need for verifiable income; credit history was unimportant, and evidence of responsible financial management was thought to be "old school" and even a bit discriminatory. The floodgates were open for homeownership, and people previously denied credit in large numbers (primarily minorities) were now the most desirable and fastest-growing customer segment in the rush to create an ownership society.

Between 2003 and 2006 subprime lending nearly doubled from $310 billion to $600 billion while total new lending dropped from $3.945 trillion to $2.980 trillion. Suddenly the subprime segment represented approximately 20 percent of all new lending, up from approximately 6 percent in 2001–2002. The fuel for this explosive growth in subprime lending came from Wall Street. Or, stated differently, it did not come from Fannie Mae and Freddie Mac—whose new lending dropped from approximately $1.4 trillion in 2002 down to $925 billion in 2006, while non-agency originations (primarily Wall Street) exploded from $414 billion in 2002 to $1.14 trillion in 2006.

The nonregulated lending community (primarily Wall Street) took the hands of naive, virginal customers who were ill prepared for the responsibilities of homeownership and who (like our hero in the song) were ridiculously outmatched by their much more experienced and manipulative counterparties. Equally important, Wall Street never intended to keep these loans on their books. They had sucker investors around the world lined up to buy this paper, encouraged to enter this club through the "fake IDs" issued by the rating agencies (S&P, Moody's, and Fitch) who assigned AAA ratings to securities backed by residential mortgages originated in an environment of the loosest lending standards in the history of US mortgage finance. These AAA ratings implied the same risk characteristics and margin of safety as lending to General Electric, ExxonMobil, or Berkshire Hathaway.

Loans for greater than 90 percent of property value shot up to more than 50 percent of new subprime originations while only about 55 percent of these borrowers provided documented evidence of their incomes; interest-only loans were now more than 25 percent (up from zero percent in 2001). Overall, underwriting was getting much looser, and the quality of borrowers was eroding dramatically, yet the AAA designations kept flowing out of the factory.

Between 1994 and 2006 approximately fifteen million new owner-occupied households were created, while only 220,000 renter households were formed during the same period, according to the US Census Bureau. The homeownership rate shot up from approximately 64 percent to 69 percent between 1994 and 2004. With "no money down" in an inflated housing market, it was only a matter of time until negative equity became the norm when the lending tide receded. And boy did it recede; it was a reverse tsunami. And all hell broke loose.

In the song, our hero came to learn that Lola was not quite who she represented, as further due diligence proved that what he thought was a *she* turned out instead to be a *he*. I hate it when that happens.

Talk about a life-altering event! Our hero had recently left home and he's finally on his own. His hormones are raging, and he captures the eye of a beautiful woman. She wants to spend more time with him, and he is overcome with desire as she invites him back to her place. Things get more intimate, and suddenly all of those clues he ignored or didn't pay attention to now make sense. Lola was a man! Assuming he doesn't go with the flow, the shock of this traumatic experience will probably take many years to overcome—much like the implosion of subprime lending.

Subprime lending dropped from a peak of $625 billion in 2005 to approximately $170 billion in 2007, a greater than 70 percent decline as defaults skyrocketed and the egregious lending practices became exposed. Wall Street origination volume was eviscerated; it dropped to approximately $300 billion in 2007 from peaks of approximately $1.2 trillion in 2005 and $1.1 trillion in 2006. Banks wrote off hundreds of billions of dollars of bad loans and began aggressively raising new money to replenish their badly depleted capital base. Thousands of people lost their jobs, with Orange County being especially hard-hit as the subprime capital of the world. Subprime was dead in terms of being a volume industry, and lending standards would remain tight for a long time as a capital-constrained banking system would have to ration capital through higher interest rates and tighter lending standards.

For CWS it was a bit of déjà vu, as we had experienced the same thing in the mobile home lending market. This industry, too, was populated by very bad actors, flush with easy money from Wall Street, who had very little knowledge about the borrowers to whom they were lending. And, most importantly, just as in the 2003–2006 period, Wall Street investment banks sold these loans to other investors.

Thus, the incentive was to generate fees based on creating paper that could be sold to others. The connection between the borrower and lender was severed, and valuable information was lost in the process. When times got tough, the losses were much greater as the terrible lending practices came to light, and there was no relationship between lender and borrower to fall back on. This process reached its peak in 1998, and ten years later the mobile home lending industry was virtually nonexistent. Capital left the industry for at least a decade, because there was no longer any trust among big institutional investors that capital could be deployed prudently on a large scale in this industry. History has proven that it could not, just as the subprime segment should never be more than 5–7 percent of the market.

As we had been saying relentlessly for a number of years, far too many people were diverted from renting into homeownership, and this had to change. It is hard to shake the "Lola" experience, and this would be the case for millions of people who should never have walked metaphorically into that club in Old Soho and bought their first home with no money down, few reserves in the bank, and using the ticking time bomb known as an adjustable-rate mortgage, merely to purchase one of the mass-produced homes that would become unavoidable money pits.

In 2007, according to the Census Bureau, owner-occupied homes dropped by approximately two hundred thousand while renter-occupied homes increased by nearly one million. It was a huge reversal and something we had been waiting to see for a number of years.

Human nature never changes. We are emotional creatures driven to extremes of fear and greed when it comes to our finances. Millions took the bait of easy money. Inexperience, someone paying attention to us for the first time, our desire for immediate gratification, and a counterparty who knew how to take advantage of all these human frailties were ingredients for the perfect toxic brew for creating ignorance and self-delusion. I would think the next time the protagonist in the song ventured into another club—if he ever did—he would be much more skeptical of any woman he meets and far more cautious in his approach to her. I believe this will also be the case with millions of Americans who were burned by rushing into homeownership.

Whereas many of the Soho clubs are still open, most of the home-market equivalents have been shut down as huge amounts of human and financial capital have exited the industry. And if our experience in the mobile home world is any indication, this will be the case for years to come.

Moral of the Story

The real lesson for me from "Lola" is about the power of deluding ourselves to see what we want to see while ignoring the disconfirming evidence. This is the confirmation bias: a natural tendency for us to take encouragement from supporting evidence while conveniently ignoring anything to the contrary.

Thank you, Lola, for helping to teach us an important lesson.

Chapter Seven

APPRECIATING THE MACRO

I would rather be vaguely right than precisely wrong.
—John Maynard Keynes

Over the years I have found that it can be highly valuable to attempt to identify major global macroeconomic trends and assess how they can impact job growth (a good proxy for real estate demand), investor sentiment (a good proxy for lender aggressiveness and its corresponding impact on new supply and investor fuel to purchase assets), and interest rates (a good proxy for the trend in capitalization rates). Some major events we've had to contend with in my career at CWS are

- the Tax Reform Act of 1986, which reversed the ability of all investors to use real estate losses to offset their ordinary income, allowing passive losses to shelter only passive gains for non–real estate professionals (the previous 1981 act had created a huge demand for real estate, while 1986 led to an exodus away from real estate);

- oil going from approximately forty dollars per barrel in the early 1980s, and to less than ten dollars in 1986 (this decimated Texas);
- the stock market crash of 1987;
- the savings and loan debacle, which led to the creation of the Resolution Trust Corporation (RTC) and the fire sale of real estate;
- the advent of securitization in the wake of the creation of the RTC to sell off and finance bulk real estate purchase;
- the near bankruptcy of the banking system (e.g., Citicorp being bailed out by Prince Al-Waleed) in 1989–90;
- the Japanese Nikkei peaking at nearly 39,000 in 1989, only to fall to less than 10,000 twenty-three years later;
- CWS's involvement in the first securitization of manufactured housing loans in 1992–1993;
- the bailout of Mexico in 1994;
- Orange County's bankruptcy in 1994;
- Japanese short-term rates dropping below 1 percent in 1995 and remaining there to this day;
- the Asian currency crisis in 1997–1998;
- the blowup of Long-Term Capital and the Russian ruble crisis in 1998;
- the implosion of manufactured home lending between 1998 and 2000;
- the tech boom and bubble bursting between 1997–2001;
- September 11, 2001;
- the US housing boom;
- subprime loans blowing up and leading to the Great Recession; and

- the Lehman Brothers bankruptcy, Bear Stearns getting taken over by JPMorgan Chase, Fannie Mae and Freddie Mac in conservatorship, and TARP, just to name some of the notable events between 2007 and 2009.

While a number of these could be covered in other parts of the book, I thought it might be informative to see what we were thinking during a few of these events and how we assessed the macro environment in terms of its potential impact on our business. The first part was written in 2004.

Sometimes we can ride a profitable wave before the excesses become so immense that they inevitably unwind and terrible losses ensue for those who were on their surfboards when the tsunami occurred. The bursting of the tech bubble in 2000–2002 turned out to be hugely impactful on our business. With the possible exception of 1990–1991 (and subsequently 2008–2013), this was the first postwar recession in which the policy response was far different from virtually all previous recessions. In the past, inflation was the biggest concern of the Federal Reserve as the economy grew relatively rapidly. The rapid growth put pressures on resources: labor, capital, and capacity utilization. This strain tended to result in an increase in inflation. In order to slow down inflationary pressures, the Federal Reserve would tighten credit and increase interest rates, with the result being a slowdown in economic activity—particularly in interest rate–sensitive industries like housing and automobiles. The country would go into recession, jobs would be lost, and then the Federal Reserve would begin loosening credit and the cycle would go in reverse.

With the bursting of the stock market bubble, however, we had a very different phenomenon. We already had a relatively low inflation rate exacerbated by the trillions of dollars lost as the NASDAQ melted down from 5,000 to below 1,200. The propensity for investors, corporations, and stock market investors to spend was diminished because of the wealth effect working in the opposite direction. As immature businesses could no longer go public, venture capital funding dried up for high-tech companies, and profitability became the most important goal. This resulted in a tremendous curtailment of capital expenditures and a wave of layoffs, which rippled through high-tech industries and impacted the entire US economy; so much of the output, particularly at the margin, was high-tech related. At the same time there was a fear that consumer spending would decrease because so much wealth had been lost in the stock market.

So what did Alan Greenspan and the Federal Reserve do? Critics of Greenspan call him a perpetual bubble blower, and that the whole name of the game in 2000, 2001, and 2002 was to buy enough time for corporate America to improve its balance sheets and earnings capability so that it could eventually spend money again on capital equipment and software and hire people again. To do this, however, the consumer sector—pretty much you and me and our friends and families—had to be propped up, and the best way of doing this was through a dramatic reduction in interest rates. The Federal Reserve lowered its benchmark federal funds rate thirteen times, from 6 percent to 1 percent, which was the lowest rate since 1958.

The mortgage market bore the brunt of the impact of this policy as lower interest rates stimulated an extraordinary amount of housing activity. The dramatic reduction in mortgage costs had numerous positive economic effects. One of these effects was to enable people to lower their monthly costs so that they could spend the savings on other areas of the economy, while another provided the opportunity to those so inclined to extract equity from their homes to pay down higher-cost debt, to improve their homes, and to save the money or spend it. Obviously a combination of all of them could happen, as well. Most importantly, cheaper, more accessible mortgage capital helped stimulate demand for housing, which propelled housing values higher and made lenders even more interested in lending against the asset—thereby stimulating further appreciation.

The key actors in making this virtuous housing circle happen were the government-sponsored enterprises (GSEs) Fannie Mae and Freddie

Mac. They became the channels through which global capital entered the US mortgage market. Assets of the GSEs plus those of the asset-backed securities and mortgage-backed securities markets had grown by over $6 trillion in slightly less than nine years (1985–1994), with most of this money entering the mortgage market.

I often ask myself the question, How long can American homeowners keep the weight of the world's economy upon their shoulders? And so far they've been able to do it remarkably well and for far longer than I would have thought. I wrote the following to our investers in 2007:

> We may have entered into a pact with the devil as we have borrowed massively from future growth in order to get through today by incurring Roaring '20s amounts of debt. There will be a day of reckoning. Unfortunately, many investors have lost a lot of money betting on a trend reversing far earlier than it actually happens. Debt growth will slow down, but you could have said that in 1982 and missed out on one of the greatest investment markets in history. At least learn this lesson: the boom of the '80s and '90s can be summed up as a massive leveraging of American businesses and households. If and when it unwinds, the opposite is virtually certain to take place. Debt reduction is bearish, while leveraging up is enormously bullish. Shrewd investors have to have an Armageddon plan to account for a massive contraction in debt in our economy and how that will impact not only households and businesses but, most importantly, lending institutions.

This turned out to be pretty prescient given the subsequent events that took place between 2007 and 2009.

Housing growth was easily the most important catalyst for keeping the economy afloat despite the stock market bubble bursting (at the turn of the century) and despite the September 11, 2001, terrorist attacks. But the question we had to ask was, Why had job growth been virtually nonexistent despite one of the greatest consumer booms in history and strong growth momentum in the economy as evidenced by the 8.2 percent GDP growth in the third quarter?

We turned to Asia for some answers, since Asia was inextricably linked to the housing boom.

Go East, Young Man

From 1995 to 2000 the US dollar appreciated dramatically in the global foreign exchange markets. Under the leadership of Treasury secretaries Robert Rubin and Lawrence Summers, the mantra was, "A strong US dollar is in the best interest of the United States." At the same time, many Asian countries such as Thailand, South Korea, Taiwan, Hong Kong, China, and Malaysia had pegged their currencies to an ultimately overvalued US dollar. Without getting into too many details, these countries attracted a lot of speculative capital flows to take advantage of very good returns inside those economies.

The speculative capital flows led to booms inside these Asian economies as more money was created to accommodate them. Eventually the booms became unsustainable. The capital flowed outward and currency crises ensued as speculators sought to sell these currencies and repatriate their money. The International Monetary Fund was brought in to bail out South Korea and Indonesia. Hong Kong had to intervene dramatically in the stock market to help prevent a meltdown there. Malaysia put forth capital controls. Chaos ensued. Indonesia had an 85 percent reduction in the value of its currency and experienced civil strife and a de facto revolution. This was very nasty business and was not without harm or ramifications.

The point of this review of history is not to focus on the details but to set forth the fact that these countries were rocked to their core. These once-in-a-lifetime experiences helped shape leaders and generations for decades to come, as the Great Depression did here in the USA. It became absolutely critical for these countries to build up very solid reserves of foreign currencies so that they would never again be subjected to such a vicious speculative attack against their domestic currencies.

So we had a philosophical requirement among Taiwan, South Korea, Hong Kong, China, Japan, Malaysia, and Singapore to build up a very strong reserve of foreign currencies. Now let's add another variable to the equation, with the opening up of China as a global economic force, particularly with its admission into the World Trade Organization (WTO). This was a monumental event that would require very significant liberalization of China's economy and certain key industries.

China, which I have visited, is an unbelievably powerful force; there is no disputing this. It is on a growth trajectory for generations to come. That's not to say that the country is not going to have financial problems, setbacks, and reversals. It surely will, particularly with such a weak banking system and lending practices. But there is really no turning back the clock on this economic monster. At the same time, however, China also had an unbelievable challenge ahead as it went through a massive restructuring of its state-owned enterprises and needed to lay off about three million people per year for at least three years. Combine this with approximately 750 million people living in the countryside who will ultimately have to migrate into the urban areas—because virtually all industrialized societies have no more than 3–10 percent of their employment in farming—and you have the makings of a potentially explosive social situation if not handled properly and delicately.

When one takes this massive potential social disruption into consideration, along with China's paramount need for social stability, it becomes clear that China will be a huge actor on the world stage for some time to come. China requires an incredible amount of private investment just to keep unemployment from growing. China's economic growth was averaging approximately 7 to 9 percent a year. With a labor force growing at only about 1 percent annually, virtually all of that growth was coming from annual productivity gains of 6 to 7 percent. China was estimated to need twenty-four million new jobs a year just to keep its unemployment rate stable (a figure that is significantly understated because there are so many migrant workers and underutilized people who truly should be counted as unemployed—*I've seen many of them with my own eyes*).

So here we were with two parts of the world going through profound transitions. The US was trying to pass the baton from corporate America to the consumer for a long enough period of time to allow corporate America to get healthy again. China was trying to transition hundreds of millions of people into free-market businesses while restructuring the state-owned enterprises that represented such a large percentage of its economy (but which were a black hole for bad loans). Add to the mix the philosophical requirement of Asian countries to build a huge war chest of foreign currency reserves with (at the time) the US strong dollar policy. This resulted in Asia building up vast foreign currency reserves by running massive trade surpluses with the US, because China had been able to export to a very consumption-oriented US economy blessed with a strong currency that allowed global goods and services to be bought relatively cheaply.

We had the making of a mercantilist situation in Asia, in which countries believe they must export their way to prosperity. This led to severe global imbalances and distortions, as ultimately the currency intervention required by the Asian countries to keep their domestic currencies weaker relative to the US dollar necessitated a significant amount of resources. It had a profound impact on our housing and mortgage markets, and this is where one had to be willing to think creatively to connect the dots.

In order to stimulate the US economy, policies emphasized consumption much more than savings. In fact, our savings rate as a country hit close to a post–World War II low. The excess consumption over savings resulted in a very large current account deficit: we were importing more goods and services than we were exporting. Without sufficient savings in our economy, this put tremendous pressure on the United States to import large amounts of capital from foreign investors.

This may sound alarming on the surface, but in the short run it was what the global economy needed, because if we think of Asia, with its desire to build up foreign currency reserves, we realize that this pressure created the necessity to focus on export-oriented industries at the expense of import-oriented consumption businesses. This resulted in Asia being more than willing to encourage, entice, and create incentives for the United States to consume more than it saved or produced. And to do this, Asia competed on price and quality. At the same time, it was willing to recycle virtually all of the dollars that it accumulated (in the foreign exchange market from its export surplus) back into the United States. The Asian countries took those dollars and invested them in US Treasury securities as well as in Fannie Mae and Freddie Mac securities, providing us with lower interest rates than would otherwise have been the case (absent Fed intervention).

Foreign custody holdings of the Federal Reserve and the Treasury and agency securities held on behalf of foreign central banks exploded to over $1.1 trillion in just a few years. These excess dollars on the global stage created pressure on the value of the US currency. There was more supply of dollars than there was demand. If the free market had been left to its own devices and not disrupted by central bank intervention, then the US dollar would have dropped rather precipitously. However, if the dollar had been allowed to float completely freely against the Japanese yen, the Chinese renminbi, and other Asian currencies, the countervailing force would have been for these currencies to appreciate rapidly. And when a currency appreciates, it puts a lot of pressure on export industries, because it makes their products more expensive to buy for weak-currency countries.

With this mercantilist philosophy so prevalent in Asia and particularly in Japan, there had been tremendous pressure on the financial authorities to rein in the depreciation of the dollar, and this intervention in the markets had taken unprecedented forms. In 2003, Japan spent over $200 billion to intervene in the foreign currency markets to buy dollars ($100 billion in January and February 2004 alone).

So where did this money go? The Asian central banks typically printed more of their domestic currency to purchase dollars and then recycle them back into US credit markets. This put downward pressure on US interest rates and strengthened our housing market, which in turn stimulated more consumption and imports of consumer goods (which helped the export industries and job growth of the Asian countries). This continued to put downward pressure on the US dollar, and required further intervention by the Asian authorities to help slow the dollar depreciation by recycling newly purchased dollars back into the US mortgage and Treasury markets. And the cycle went on and on while the imbalances continued to grow. Our claims to foreign creditors continued to increase at a very rapid rate as we exported manufacturing jobs overseas.

The logical, absurd extreme of this whole game was as follows. The United States would become the least wealthy nation with the highest standard of living: everyone lived in very large homes and had access to tremendous consumer goods and services. Meanwhile Japan would become the largest global creditor and wealthiest nation in the world, but with the lowest standard of living: its citizens would survive on rice and would live in very small houses. Obviously this was absurd, but an extreme example of how it could end. Bringing the analogy up to date (2015), just substitute China for Japan.

There had been no effort at rebalancing by either global monetary authorities (with the possible exception of the European Central Bank) or the Bush administration. I had a very hard time seeing how we could rebalance without a lot of pain, because no major country seemed to want to have a strong currency, and we therefore ran the risk of beggar-thy-neighbor policies, whereby countries would embark upon competitive currency devaluations in order to keep their export markets alive.

The goal was the debasement of currencies by central bankers around the world. Any way you looked at it, virtually all the major central banks were in a reflation mode.

The US had unbelievable fiscal and monetary stimulus taking place. The Federal Reserve kept short-term interest rates below the rate of inflation, which was inherently inflationary. The Asian countries that were trying to weaken their currencies found themselves printing more local currency to buy dollars. So the $64,000 question was, Why did we keep choosing variable-rate loans when most indicators pointed to higher interest rates in the future?

I won't go into too much detail here, but the key factor was that fixed-rate financing represented too much of an insurance policy—with the starting interest rate advantage so strong compared with fixed-rate financing (approximately 2 percent), and with long-term interest rate caps (below 7 percent) and prepayment flexibility. Our financial structure offered a low enough cost of capital that it represented a very good risk/reward trade-off. With that being said, I believed that the financial markets at some point (probably within five to seven years) were at risk of a major "financial accident" that could have an impact on interest rates. But that is where our interest rate cap would come into play. (This turned out to be an accurate prognostication as well.)

The Year Ahead

In this historic account, the "year ahead" that I'm talking about is 2004. So what did it all mean for our strategy? Obviously, financing was an important component. We decided to continue to look for properties that were well located and had attractive going-in yields that could be financed with variable-rate loans having interest rate caps. At the same time, we would continue to consider selling every property that had a loan maturing. We would always ask the question of whether this was a good time to sell, because (as mentioned previously) delivering an unencumbered property to the marketplace would have potentially tremendous value for investors who could access the same low-cost capital that we could.

It was important that we continued to have investment themes guiding our strategy from a macroeconomic perspective. I will summarize these:

- We considered that defense spending was not only here to stay, but should continue to grow. So we would focus on locations that had exposure to defense businesses, such as Fort Worth, Texas.

- The weak dollar was part of the economic policy of the Bush administration. It should have stimulated older-economy manufacturing, export-oriented businesses despite long-term trends going against them. It should also have encouraged foreign manufacturers to open up facilities in the United States, with the most prominent being Toyota's enormous investment in San Antonio at over $800 million.

- Another key theme was the recovery of capital spending. Companies were letting their capital equipment depreciate at a much more rapid rate than it was being replaced. This could only go on for so long before productive capacity was diminished. I expected to see a growing expenditure by corporate America on technology equipment and software, so that it would no longer be a drag on the economy and would be a source of economic growth. This would help Dallas, Austin, Raleigh, and Denver, and would assist in positioning our markets for relatively stronger economic growth than other areas of the country. We intended to look selectively at acquisitions in these markets.

As always, we found ourselves left with more questions than answers. Could corporate America provide enough growth in the event that the American consumer had to de-leverage and therefore spend less? Could the US avoid a significant economic contraction if and when debt growth slowed down or was reduced? Could China, Japan, and the United States all create sustainable economic growth despite the enormous imbalances their policies were creating? Could China maintain social stability by restructuring its state-owned enterprises and continue to attract enough capital to produce large numbers of new jobs? When would Asian central banks begin to realize that currency intervention is ultimately futile? What would this do to the global economy? Would I be able to get over the pain of the last few years? I guess only God, therapists, and brilliant, independent-minded thinkers could see how all of the pieces would fit together—and you, dear readers, with the benefit of your post-2004, perfect hindsight.

Chapter Eight

JACOB—ONE IN A MILLION

The events that one recalls from early life are generally happy ones such as birthdays and anniversaries (including our own wedding anniversaries, if we intend to stay married). But sometimes, everything doesn't go according to plan. May 23, 1995, marks an event in my life that wasn't supposed to happen. I learned a lot that day, and it taught me a great deal about the nature of risk and uncertainty and how things can go terribly wrong for entirely unexpected reasons. This journey down the road of risk and uncertainty is a very personal one, but one that I believe is informative nonetheless.

I will never forget getting the call. I was in a meeting in our office and I was suddenly paged over our loudspeaker that I had a call. I ignored it, because I didn't want to interrupt the meeting. When I didn't pick up, the receptionist came into the room and said that I needed to talk to the person on hold, because there was a problem at home. I excused myself and picked up my phone to find my wife, Roneet, at the other end of the line. She had just gotten a call from our babysitter, who had said that Jacob (our twenty-five-month-old son) had vomited, was very irritable, and was simply not acting like his typical self (i.e., wild and crazy). Although we had just had the house painted—so it might just have been a violent reaction to the paint fumes—Roneet was concerned enough to call 911.

I went straight to the hospital and on arrival found Jacob being evaluated by an emergency room doctor. Roneet told me that the paramedics were pretty dismissive of her concerns, that it was probably just the flu, and that she was essentially an overreactive mother. The emergency room doctor concurred and decided that he was going to release Jacob.

Still perplexed by Jacob's disorientation and believing that he needed further evaluation, we took him immediately to his pediatrician for a second opinion. She checked him out to see if his condition was impacting his balance and then told us to take him home—to watch him closely, and to report back if nothing improved. Still shaken and with an innate sense that something wasn't quite right, we did as the pediatrician advised.

As the day progressed, Jacob slept a lot, and when he was awake he continued to be very irritable. Day turned into night, and he just wasn't getting better. We began to notice that one side of his mouth was beginning to droop a little. We called the pediatrician, a different one who was on call because ours was now done for the day. We told him about Jacob's condition and what we were seeing happen to his face. "Take him immediately to CHOC," he said. CHOC is the Children's Hospital of Orange County and it's only ten minutes from our house. This obviously frightened us as we were both pretty young (thirty and thirty-one) and Jacob was our first child. Roneet and I had both lived pretty blessed lives in which fortune shined through so often while misfortune was a rarity. Such a situation was therefore very unfamiliar.

Along with Roneet's father, a great person to have on your side during trying times, we immediately headed out to our car for the drive to CHOC's emergency room. Upon hearing our description of the symptoms, the doctor called a neurologist and ordered an MRI of Jacob's brain. The memory of accompanying Jacob through the cavernous and sterile halls of the hospital basement to get to the MRI room is etched on my brain. It seemed surreal that, at only two years old, Jacob was being taken through a hospital that was connected to the St. Joseph Hospital that caters to older patients.

Once the photos were taken, all we could do was wait while we contemplated the fact that Jacob had always been such a healthy child. The only meaningful ailment that I could remember him having was the chickenpox a couple of months earlier, and even that was a very mild case. I couldn't think of any possible cause for Jacob's malaise other than the paint fumes at home. I hoped that the MRI would be fine and we would soon be back to normal. And then I felt a hand on my shoulder.

I turned around to see the very pleasant grandfatherly face of the pediatrician who was on call, a man our family had known for many years. I was surprised to see him there with the emergency room doctor. "We've found something," he said. My heart sank. "Jacob suffered a stroke."

How could I ever describe my reaction to this news? Our two-year-old baby, this precious ball of joy and love who brought such incredible happiness to our lives, had suffered a stroke. It was incomprehensible. The thoughts began to race, and the questions spewed forth. How bad? Was he going to be okay? Will he be brain damaged? Will he walk? Will he talk? Will he be able to move his hand? Will he lead an independent life? *Will he live?* Of course, no one could answer any of these questions.

Into the Tunnel of Uncertainty

Jacob was moved immediately to the pediatric intensive care unit to be monitored constantly. No family member ever left Jacob's side other than when Roneet and I slept in the waiting room at night. I was getting used to the nurses' early morning routine checks on Jacob, when—one time— it was not so routine. The nurse woke Jacob up and shined the light into his eyes, but he was not responding like he had been. She started saying "Jacob, can you hear me? Jacob! Jacob!" She began to shake him to see how he would react. He was limp. She called the emergency room doctor immediately, and he didn't like what he saw.

"Jacob, buddy, can you hear me? Can you hear me, buddy?" (He was always very cute in how he interacted with Jacob.)

No reaction.

It was like a scene from the television show *ER*. The doctor told everybody to get out. Jacob was developing severe swelling in his brain that was very dangerous. We were shuttled off into a room and asked to sign a consent form on the spot, allowing him to be operated on if necessary. They induced him to slip into a coma so they could hook him up to the necessary equipment and put a shunt into his head to drain the fluid and help slow the swelling.

Eventually the fluid was drained in a procedure that fully displayed the capacity of an individual to be completely focused and in the moment. The neurosurgeon showed extraordinary mastery of what I'm sure was an easy procedure for him. Now came the anguish of waiting to see if Jacob would awake from the coma, and if so, what state he would be in. During a quiet period I asked the doctor how serious it was when the swelling started building up; he said that Jacob would have been within thirty minutes of death if they hadn't intervened. That's all I needed to know in order to appreciate the gravity of the situation.

After approximately three days in a coma, Jacob awoke. While still irritable and groggy, we could see a lot of the old Jacob returning. After eight days in the intensive care unit and fourteen in total at the hospital, Jacob was being discharged. With a partially shaved head, a severe limp in his left leg, and minimal use of his left hand, Jacob was finally returning home.

The Comeback Kid

To make a long story short, Jacob made a remarkable recovery. His cognition was strong, he started doing well in school, and with speech therapy he made great improvement in his language skills. Despite his dream of one day playing in either the NBA or the major leagues, he will always have physical challenges; he still walks with a bit of a limp and has very little fine motor movement in his left hand. Despite this adversity, or maybe because of it, he continues to have an extraordinary spirit, great sense of humor, and a wonderfully cheerful and positive attitude. He is also a college graduate, and pretty good-looking kid (thanks to his mother).

So what caused Jacob's stroke? After very extensive testing of his heart and blood, doctors concluded that his very mild case of chickenpox was actually quite virulent. It turns out that Jacob's immune system was so strong that he produced an overabundance of antibodies to the *varicella* (chickenpox) virus that ended up forming a clot, stopping his blood from flowing to his brain. For children aged fourteen and under, the annual incidence rate for strokes is about 2.52 per 100,000 per year, according to a study by the Mayo Clinic. I now looked at the world from a totally different perspective on many levels, especially with regard to risk.

One surface-level lesson is that devastating things can happen out of the blue. Such events are what the financial philosopher Nassim Nicholas Taleb describes as "black swan" events:

> Black swan events are events that are simply not meant to happen, but which do happen more regularly and more devastatingly than you might imagine. They get their name from the fact that, for many centuries, Europeans thought that all swans were white and that black swans simply didn't exist. Until the whole apple cart was upset in 1697 when a Dutch explorer discovered black swans in Western Australia.

Bad things can happen to good people. That's a fact of life and there's nothing we can do about it. Yet, when I think more deeply about Jacob's stroke, I realize it was not a purely random event. I must admit that when he got the mild case of chickenpox I was actually somewhat happy, because I believed that he could now be done with this at a very young age and never have the risk of experiencing it as an adult when it can be much more serious. I mentally chose short-term pain in order to avoid the possibility of greater pain in the future. What I underestimated, however, was that this virus was not benign at all. It's actually quite powerful and can cause a multitude of unexpected problems, as we came to realize later. I learned the very painful lesson that exposing oneself or others to risk is something of which I should be consciously aware, and that there should be compensation for taking on such exposure. Just because nothing adverse happens one time, it doesn't mean that it was the right decision to expose oneself to such risk in the first place. Another way of looking at it is from the opposite perspective: if I never have to make a claim on an insurance policy, it doesn't mean that the insurance should never have been purchased. One never knows. As Socrates would have said: "The only thing I know is that I do not know." The Socratic method of questioning and admission of ignorance is our only defense against the delusion that we know something completely and truly.

Jacob's exposure to the chickenpox introduced a set of circumstances that created what Mark Buchanan, author of *Ubiquity: Why Catastrophes Happen*, identified as "fingers of instability." While we never know what will eventually cascade into a catastrophe—whether it be a stock market crash, earthquake, forest fire, avalanche, or war—the presence of unstable forces builds up over time to create an environment in which such devastations can occur. Buchanan labels this the "critical state."

Understanding Unpredictability

Although they are rare, many natural events follow what mathematicians call a "power law." When power laws are in force, large events happen far less frequently than small ones, according to a fixed ratio. For example, the frequency of earthquakes drops by a factor of four for each doubling of released energy. Let's say that very small earthquakes with an energy level of 100 (arbitrary value) take place 1,000 times per year on average around the world. Under this formula, earthquakes with a value of 200 would take place only 250 times per year (on average) and those with a value of 400 would occur only 63 times per year (on average). And so on.

One of the lessons from power laws is that extreme events ("black swans") occur more frequently than traditional statistical analysis and intuition would lead us to believe. Examples include the 9.0 earthquake that led to the tsunamis in Indonesia and other Asian countries, Hurricanes Katrina, Rita, and Andrew, and the devastating fires in Yellowstone in 1988. Financial examples include the stock market crash of 1987, the Asian currency crisis in 1997, and the Russian default of 1998 and subsequent collapse of Long-Term Capital Management.

By studying daily changes in the value of stock indices, the stock market crash in October 1987 should have taken place only once in four million years, yet similar extremes have been witnessed more regularly than that in the course of the past one hundred years. Thus, there must be something wrong with our traditional ways of evaluating risk. And indeed there is, because of a phenomenon known as "fat tails" whereby extreme outcomes are more common than your standard normal distribution. Beware black swans with fat tails!

According to Didier Sornette, a UCLA professor and author of *Why Stock Markets Crash*, analyzing daily price movements independently is sufficient 99 percent of the time. In other words, tomorrow's price movements should have very little correlation with today's. The other 1 percent of the time, however, is when everything goes haywire, because suddenly very strong dependencies develop between successive trading days such that they feed off each other and can lead to the kind of 30 percent drop over a four-day period that occurred in October 1987. According to Sornette, the largest sell-offs during these extremes occur about one hundred times more often than they should.

The key is to identify the conditions that make markets susceptible to such dramatic shifts, or the "critical state," as Buchanan labels it. The article "Hedge Funds Hit Rough Weather but Stay Course," published in the *Wall Street Journal* on June 22, 2006, speaks to this very well:

> Risk models tend to underestimate how hard it is to get out of a market when the exits are stuffed with folks trying to do the same thing. "You can't stress test a crowded trade," said Bradley Ziff, who led the Mercer Oliver Wyman study. "Everyone is worried about how to handle a situation when everyone piles in."

I think this summarizes what Sornette is trying to convey. Most of the time it's business as usual, but on very rare occasions there can be a run on the bank, which can lead to devastating consequences. When a mass of people in a crowded theater can only get out of one small door via one aisle, carnage can ensue as a result of one man's ill-timed cry of "Fire!" even if made in jest.

Sornette's research has concluded that approximately two-thirds of all dramatic crashes (or "shocks," as he likes to label them) can be attributed to an endogenous origin and can be identified by the pattern of a long period of optimistic price increases followed by a blow-off phase of huge appreciation. During this blow-off phase there is great public participation by the "common man" while experts justify extreme valuations through explanations that we are "in a new economy," "in the midst of an information revolution," "witnessing a new paradigm," or simply "this time it's different." Eventually something causes the market to collapse under its own weight, and the 99 percent normal behavior is superseded by the highly correlated 1 percent environment in which selling leads to more selling. The key is to not be too conservative when we're in a 99 percent environment and to not get wiped out by the 1 percent event.

One of the most important lessons I've learned in the investment world is that stability breeds instability (thank you, Hyman Minsky). Long periods of prosperity and success lead to greater confidence and to investors taking on more and more risk. Because it has paid to do so in the past, it will presumably continue to do so into the future. More leverage builds up in the system, and asset prices can go beyond their intrinsic values based on fundamentals like earnings, cash flow, and book value. This creates an unstable foundation in which ownership is in weak hands.

An Overdue Thanks

Returning to the original topic of this chapter, I'd like to conclude on a personal note by saying a big "thank you" to my son, Jacob. Well, Jacob, I know you have gone through a lot, but you've sure put Mom and me through the wringer as well. But I must say thank you for showing me how precious life is and how every day we have a choice as to how we can respond to events in our lives. You have taught me that allowing adversity to get us down is a choice, and we don't have to respond that way. By taking ownership of the challenges we face, we open ourselves up to having choices, and with choice comes control of the ultimate outcome. Of course there are still days when I feel like I'm under assault from all directions. But then I take a deep breath, think of your laugh and your zest for life, and I start to feel much better, more in control. I develop a much healthier perspective on my challenges.

You have also helped me in business, because I know the unexpected can happen, and that we must always avoid being in the "critical state" so that we can weather any storm. Someday the music will stop, and I want to make sure that CWS and our investors will always have a chair to sit on when that happens. Thank you, and I hope that I can teach you as much as you have taught me.

The moral of this story—or rather, these stories—is that economic (and other) shocks can occur at any time for no apparent reason, other than the fact that things have apparently been going so right for so long. Expect the unexpected.

September 11

There can be no greater black swan event than the event that took place on September 11, 2001—the day that most of us will never forget.

While many have characterized the events of 9/11 as a tragedy, I respectfully disagree. The outcome may have been inhumanely tragic, but the events themselves were pure, unadulterated evil carried out by weak, despicable individuals under the influence of demagogues using religion to justify a perverse life focused on destruction. Many events in life have unintended consequences, and the terrorist attacks on the World Trade Center and the Pentagon are no exception. Despite an apparently cynical, materialistic, and divided society, the perpetrators didn't realize that most of us truly love this great country of ours and yearn to give something back to the nation and to our fellow citizens.

The terrorists did not realize that most of us view our material lives as byproducts of a brilliantly conceived system that seeks to protect the rights of individuals (even if they disagree with the majority) through the rule of law. The more liberty, the greater opportunity there is for us to ascertain the needs and wants of our fellow global citizens and to work hard to satisfy those wants by engaging in business and social services. Through hard work and risk taking we expect to earn rewards, if we are successful in our endeavors. The system is not perfect: some people fall through the cracks, and some risk-takers and suppliers of capital are over-compensated for their contributions. But for the most part the capitalist system has dramatically improved the lives of our citizens. No system is perfect, but if immigration is any indicator of the attractiveness of living and working in the United States, then we are by far the best country in the world for providing equal opportunities regardless of race, religion, or creed.

The response to September 11 was not based on our fear that our toys would be taken away, but rather that the system that made those toys possible was at risk. Citizens from all backgrounds united to show our faith in a system that has improved the lives of so many. We all recognize that no house is safe or worth living in if it doesn't have a solid foundation. When the core of who we are is at stake, nothing takes on more importance. The time for petty politics and social preaching was over; seriousness and dedication to a larger cause—the perpetuation of freedom—was now of utmost importance. Baby Boomers, it turns out, were not so self-absorbed after all. We realized that there are causes greater than ourselves, and that we should "bear any burden, pay any price," in the words of John F. Kennedy.

As the President stated at the time, one of the best ways to show the world that we were still in control was to get on with our normal lives. With this in mind, it was important for us to consider where we were headed and how this would impact our investments at CWS.

Without question, the economic growth that was already stalling went backwards after September 11. Consumer confidence had been shaken, and when combined with a decimated technology sector—stemming from almost nonexistent corporate capital spending—this produced some challenging times for us to face. Even after nine interest-rate cuts, the stock market had still not recovered: a historical anomaly and ominous sign. The obvious bright spots were extremely low short-term interest rates (which made holding cash more painful for savers, so they might as well spend it) and government spending (for defense, security, and rebuilding in New York). Defense spending could not have come at a better time for laid-off technology workers, who would now be able to find homes at defense contractors like Boeing, Northrup Grumman, and

TRW. While this seemed to bode well for California, we still needed to work off some excesses built up from 1996 through 2000.

With the challenging economic environment and difficult technology job market, a number of high-paying jobs had been lost. This created a much more price-conscious consumer, aggressively seeking to minimize his monthly expenditures. When this consumer psychology was combined with nervous developers worried about leasing up their apartment communities to be able to refinance their construction loans, it created a much more competitive operating environment—particularly in north Austin and Denver, where many tech companies had been shedding jobs.

We are always concerned when new developments are leasing up in softening demand markets, because nervous developers make self-serving, short-term pricing decisions that can exacerbate market weakness. They have no problem offering two months' free rent in order to fill an unoccupied apartment. They do this because when it comes time to refinance their construction loans with new lenders, these units become occupied by residents paying market rents after their move-in specials have expired. Unfortunately, current residents of existing apartment communities use this information as negotiating leverage when it comes time to renew their leases. The end result is pressure to lower rents for existing residents to entice them to stay. The other option is to call their bluff and let them go through the hassle of moving. Usually there's a compromise in between.

Given the competitive landscape described above, our distribution policy going forward was quite conservative. We decided to distribute based on conservative assumptions. We realized that in some cases this could lead to a reduction in distributions, particularly for those properties that were scheduled to convert from interest-only debt service payments to both principal and interest within the next couple of years. This change would lead to a significant increase in debt service, as a portion of the loan got repaid each month. While this built up investor equity, it also consumed current cash by increasing our fixed charges.

Economics dictates that markets cannot remain perpetually overbuilt, because the returns generated from building new apartments is too low to justify the risk. With this in mind, we wanted to stay on a solid enough financial footing to remain strong when the markets turned as supply dried; we wanted to capture the above-average returns that always result when demand exceeds supply. Virtually every rental housing market in the country was challenged. Even in Orange County, which had a strong housing market, Irvine Apartment Communities initiated 6 percent rent reductions for long-term residents to entice them to stay on when their leases expired. In addition, they were no longer contemplating building any new communities other than those currently already under construction—despite a virtual monopoly on the Irvine Ranch. We are aware of properties in the Bay Area whose market rents had dropped by 33 percent in less than one year (boy, how times have changed).

We were clearly at a point in the cycle where it paid to be very conservative. We also believed that some terrific buying opportunities would occur in the course of the subsequent couple of years, particularly in north Austin, where a fair amount of new product was coming out of the ground. Weak developers without staying power in a challenging market could be forced to sell at a discount to replacement cost. Historically, our best purchases have come at times of uncertainty and economic difficulty. Although we saw some more realistic pricing among sellers, it still did not match our more conservative view of the future. This is partly attributable to low interest rates (which enable purchasers to pay higher prices because of the lower cost of capital), the presence of numerous buyers (such as pension funds and REITs), and a healthy banking system that was still making capital available to quality borrowers. At this point, we were not seeing anything that was approaching what took place in the early 1990s, when real estate values plummeted and led to the creation of the RTC by the government.

Throughout the history of our amazing country, each time we have faced a challenge we have come out stronger and better than if we had never experienced it at all. A free society and a free economy allows entre-preneurs, risk-takers, and capital providers to muster the resources neces-sary to overcome the challenge, because they can earn sufficient rewards to compensate them for coming up with creative solutions to whatever obstacles they face. The point is that we have an entire economy dedicated to organizing people, capital, and equipment so as to produce goods and services that enable us to improve our lives and business practices. We use our brains, technology, and capital to improve our nation's security. Although it doesn't happen overnight, any downturn eventually ends and long-term growth resumes. It's never good to bet against America.

While it is natural to take a conservative stance when times are tough, the big rewards can be attained by bravely betting on the eventual (and inevitable) recovery. Or, as Warren Buffett—the Oracle of Omaha—might say: "Be fearful when others are greedy and greedy when others are fearful!"

Taking Advantage of Opportunities

I have alluded to the black swan event that occurred on September 11, 2001: the event that ultimately led (rightly or wrongly) to the invasion of Iraq and the second Gulf War.

It is hard to overstate how impressive the initial victory in Iraq—in approximately three weeks—actually was. Coalition casualties were very low despite the vast territory (including urban areas) captured in such a short period of time. Such success could not have come about without tremendous technological improvements since the first Gulf War.

In a speech to the American Society of News Editors on April 9, 2003, Vice President Dick Cheney said the following:

> Having been involved in planning and waging the Persian
> Gulf War in 1991 as Secretary of Defense, I think I can say
> with some authority that this campaign has displayed vastly

improved capabilities, far better than we did a dozen years ago. In Desert Storm, only 20 percent of our air-to-ground fighters could guide a laser-guided bomb to target. Today, all of our air-to-ground fighters have that capability. In Desert Storm, it usually took up to two days for target planners to get a photo of a target, confirm its coordinates, plan the mission, and deliver it to the bomber crew. Now we have near real-time imaging of targets with photos and coordinates transmitted by e-mail to aircraft already in flight. In Desert Storm, battalion, brigade and division commanders had to rely on maps, grease pencils and radio reports to track the movements of our forces. Today our commanders have a real-time display of our own forces on their computer screens. In Desert Storm, we did not yet have the B-2. But that aircraft is now critical to our operations. And on a single bombing sortie, a B-2 can hit 16 separate targets, each with a 2,000-pound, precision-guided, satellite-based weapon. . . . Bottom line, with less than half of the ground forces and two-thirds of the air assets used 12 years ago in Desert Storm, Secretary Rumsfeld and General Franks have achieved a far more difficult objective.[1]

At CWS we had been communicating to our investors our bullishness on defense as a growth industry. No pun intended, but at the time it didn't take a rocket scientist to figure out that vast resources would be invested in defense for the foreseeable future. The facts cited in Vice President Cheney's speech showed the incredible power of matching technology with a well-trained military. We knew of no other industry with such visibility for producing a large number of high-quality jobs in the

---

1. Vice President Dick Cheney, Speech to The American Society of Newspaper Editors, April 9, 2003. http://www.nytimes.com/2003/04/09/international/worldspecial/09TEXT-CHENEY.html.

next five years, particularly as corporate America continued to restructure through cost cutting and capacity reduction. For these reasons we aggressively pursued two acquisitions in Fort Worth in 2002, near the Lockheed Martin manufacturing plant that won the $200+ billion Joint Strike Fighter contract. This program rapidly bore fruit, with Lockheed being awarded a $6 billion contract with funding committed through 2013, and with Lockheed hiring hundreds of workers in response.

But wait!

Investors should always question the premise whenever an investment thesis is presented. After all, we believed that having exposure to cities with a large number of technology jobs would produce good returns for our investors. While Cheney's speech shows the incredible power of technology and that it is undoubtedly here to stay, our thesis didn't anticipate the total collapse of the investment market and how that would decimate technology jobs. That correction was terribly painful for cities like Austin, Denver, and Raleigh.

So, what about defense? What premises was I working from that made me reasonably confident in my thesis? After all, many people were confident about technology, and that turned out to be problematic with the exception (ironically) of those firms with defense exposure. Well, I based our strategy on the Bush Doctrine and the fact that defending the homeland required an entire retooling of our security infrastructure to either preempt threats or detect them early enough to prevent widespread damage. I saw technology as an important component of each.

As previously mentioned, one of my most important investment principles comes from George Soros, who believes that you can't divorce the observer from the observed. In other words, the very act of inserting oneself into the observation process changes what is observed. The Bush Doctrine was a perfect example. In a world of weapons of mass destruction that can be easily proliferated, the Bush Doctrine made no distinction between those who commit terrorism and those who harbor terrorists. It sought to take the war outside of the United States and it would not wait for irrefutable proof of an imminent threat before taking action. It also endorsed the idea that, ultimately, only democratic forms of government can stop states from sponsoring terrorism. The policy was largely about looking for problems rather than waiting for them to become apparent, which was an example of the observer (President Bush and his national security team) influencing what is observed (potential threats to the United States). Just like a hypochondriac patient, it is easier to find problems—or think you see problems—when you are looking for them.

With such a preemptive strategy, the entire doctrine was based on attacking threats before they became large enough to undercut our military advantage. President Bush had already proven that he would not base the United States' security on hoping and waiting, even if it came at the expense of international relations. It was more important for him to take action ahead of concrete proof rather than sit in a circle at the United Nations, holding hands with the other members, singing "Kumbaya," and throwing bones of appeasement to dictators. Playtime was over, because the cost of waiting for definitive proof would subject us to nuclear blackmail or a terrorist attack on our civilian population with weapons of mass destruction.

So, I worked from the premise that the Bush administration saw the world through a prism of good and evil. Evil exists, would continue to exist, and must be confronted head-on with all of our economic and military power. Only through strength could dictatorial regimes be forced to change; only through democracy could they change permanently. This was bullish for defense.

Another important lesson in life and investing is to force oneself to think of the unintended consequences of a decision or policy. The most obvious unintended consequences for the Bush Doctrine were that it would either

- (a) degenerate into paranoia: seeing risks everywhere and completely overstretching our military commitments across the globe until we become too spread out and ineffective; or

- (b) cause the opposite of what it was intended to do: encouraging the proliferation of WMDs and terrorism rather than stopping them (for example, North Korea and Iran would arguably have nothing to lose by arming and terrorizing).

Successful investing requires a cold calculation of risks and rewards. I believed that the Bush Doctrine was necessary, ultimately, in order to make the world a safer place. But I also believed that it could create more instability in the shorter term, which would mean a continued increase in defense spending—particularly for high-tech weaponry (the jury is still out).

I was minded to think that if the unintended consequences did play out, then this would serve to make the Bush administration even more aggressive in applying its doctrine. In a similar vein, the next unintended consequence is that dictatorships would become even more dictatorial as they offered very little material progress for their citizens, and as the rise of democracy signaled the end of their regimes. History is not kind to regimes of terror that loosen the reins of control, which may explain why (more recently) Bashar Al-Assad tightened his grip on Syria in the face of internal and international opposition.

I reckoned that the Middle East was set to get very messy, which would mean more suicide bombers and snipers targeting US troops and undermining Iraq's movements toward democracy. Because no country could defeat us militarily, our enemies' biggest hope would be to strike fear in us (at home and abroad) in order to cause our economy to freeze. Another 9/11 could have rocked our economy unimaginably, and for this reason I believed that extraordinary resources would be invested to increase law enforcement agencies' abilities to track individuals or groups who were cooking up homegrown biological or chemical weapons.

What can we conclude from all this? Rather than our extraordinary military victory forcing terrorists and rogue states to act in ways we wanted them to act, it could have had the opposite effect in the short run. Expect the unexpected. That's why I remained bullish on defense spending, while being aware that I could have been wrong.

No matter how logical and rational your political or investment hypothesis is, you must account for the fact that your own actions (or those of others) can cause things to get worse in the short term before they get better. This is the law of unintended consequences.

So there you have it. Approximately forty-two years of my life (at the time this was written) encapsulated in a way to show how CWS and I got to the point in 2008 where the world was seemingly going to hell in a handbasket and we were working through a number of issues related to property loans during a time when lenders were having federal regulators breathing down their necks, making loan modifications quite challenging. Yet, we also knew that it was times like these that could offer some of the best investment opportunities for many years to come. I have shown you how my personal wiring and interests along with the great partnership among Steve, Mike, and me, along with our very talented CWS organization, combined with our invaluable experience, gave us the tools, mental construct, and psychological makeup to take a step back and see if we were on the verge of a Munger Moment. What follows is a very detailed and, I believe, fascinating and unique case study of how we transformed wisdom into wealth amid the carnage of the Great Recession.

As for those two properties we purchased in Fort Worth, we sold one in 2014, generating an annual return of over 15 percent per year during the twelve-year holding period and a cumulative return of 3.4 times one's original investment. We still own the second one, and it has returned 177 percent of one's original investment while being worth substantially more than what was invested. It is generating annual distributions in excess of 10 percent of the original investment, despite having had a significant percentage of the original capital returned via previous refinances.

Part II

CWS'S
MUNGER MOMENT

Chapter Nine

INTRODUCTION

Nobody puts Baby in a corner!
—*Johnny Castle, in* Dirty Dancing

Between 2003 and 2007, the heyday of the housing boom, we at CWS had been aggressively buying apartment communities to bolster our portfolio. We were also selling quite a few properties, as Wall Street was lending aggressively and fueling enormous demand for apartments. The investment banking firms had become a more permanent fixture in the real estate market through their aggressive issuance of commercial mortgage-backed securities (CMBS) fueled by enormous global demand for this paper. Now, even the least sophisticated investor could get access to capital—though we all know what eventually happened because of that.

During this time there was also a tremendous amount of money raised by syndicators tapping a growing pool of investors who had recently sold property. As discussed earlier, there is a component of the tax law called the "1031 exchange" that allows investors to defer gains on the sale of a piece of real estate if they reinvest those dollars in other real estate within six months of the original sale (it is more complicated than that, but this is a workable summary). These syndicators leveraged the fact that these recent sellers had money they needed to plow back into real estate to defer paying Uncle Sam his due. But these syndicators also charged enormous fees and bought properties at wildly inflated prices—which was truly doing a disservice to these people who were trying to turn their gains into a source of passive income.

To be truthful, we monetized some of this madness by selling some of our properties to syndicators—many of whom got hit hard by the coming recession and housing crash that arrived in late 2007.

Of course, the Great Recession, as it has been widely dubbed, wasn't our first experience with a downturn. CWS had been hit hard during the recession of the late 1980s to early 1990s, and again from 2001 to 2003. But each experience was unique in the lessons it taught us.

For example, the recession that began in 2001 after the dot-com meltdown impacted us because people still had jobs and access to credit, so they were drawn to buy homes rather than rent our apartments—a confluence of factors that put pressure on our occupancy rates and hence our cash flow.

But the recession that commenced in 2007 was different; it didn't significantly affect our operating income. The real challenge for CWS was that we had about fifteen key loans coming due just as the banking industry was brought to its knees by the blowup of the subprime mortgage market. Banks were suffering and were forced to turn to bailout money from the government, which subjected them to intense scrutiny by federal regulators.

This combination of factors created significant hurdles for us to be able to renew the loans that were coming due in 2009–2010. Most of the lenders required repayment of some of the principal as a condition to granting extensions. This was particularly challenging, since many of these properties were purchased with GE Capital as our principal equity partner at a time when GE Capital was under enormous financial pressure. An important lesson we learned is the value of teaming up with partners who have financial strength when times get tough. While that was a difficult time, we were able to convince our lenders to allow us to make additional capital contributions in order to get the loan extensions we needed. This was a milder version of the Cataclysmic Interface, since we were dealing with corporate money as opposed to individuals' funds.

We also concurrently faced additional challenges with our two biggest lenders, Fannie Mae and Freddie Mac, the quasi-government entities that are so essential to keeping liquidity flowing in the apartment market throughout all cycles. Both organizations were now taking a much closer look at our real estate portfolio. In what proved to be an initially disadvantageous move, we laid out for them in great detail our loan maturities and cash flows relative to debt service. Our schedules, it turned out, were far more detailed than our competitors' and revealed all of the loan maturities that were approaching, and these two lenders were very concerned. We were initially penalized by being the first mover, since they didn't have nearly as much information about their other borrowers' portfolios as they did about our properties. We were able to turn that challenge into an advantage, though, because our comprehensive reporting clearly pointed out the challenges we were facing and also that we had a plan for each one. And when we successfully resolved all of them, our lenders were simply amazed.

From a broader perspective, CWS was facing a Munger Moment, and we were fortunate to have the resources to take advantage of the opportunities that began to unfold before us because of our past patience and prudence.

Because we had staying power, thanks to our investors and strong lending relationships, we could look at the unfolding market in a far different way than many others were seeing it. A lot of firms seemed to be leaning in the same direction: playing defense versus focusing on growth because of the problems they had to contend with and because of insufficient access to growth capital.

If you only play defense then you are unlikely to look objectively and optimistically at the potential opportunities around you. We, on the other hand, were prepared to take advantage of what turned out to be a market filled with tremendous buying opportunities—perhaps one that would turn out to be a once-in-a-lifetime event in terms of the rewards it offered relative to the risk incurred.

The key questions for us were, What was going to happen to our net operating income (NOI), and what was going to happen to our cost of capital?

Learning from the Past

We knew from history that in times of recession, the government typically looks to stimulate the housing market as a way to jump-start the economy. But, in this case, with the housing market at the epicenter of the financial meltdown, we knew that it would likely become more difficult to buy homes. This, we thought, would stimulate demand for flexible housing solutions, such as apartments, that would allow people to move to the areas where the jobs were while also helping them to build and rebuild their credit without being tied to a costly, illiquid asset. In addition, the increasing desire among young people for vibrant, urban living also positioned apartments for more demand.

We also knew that lenders would be tightening up their lending to single-family and multifamily builders, thereby constricting the supply of new homes and apartments.

We believed strongly that we had a good handle on supply. But what would happen to demand, which was largely a function of jobs? We also needed to understand what would happen to interest rates, which is a large factor (though not the only one) in determining the cost of capital.

There was so much pessimism in 2008 and 2009, because people thought the world was going into the abyss. There was also quite a bit of concern about skyrocketing interest rates, because we were supposedly beholden to China and Japan to buy our Treasuries to help fund our spiraling deficits.

That meant that most people in our situation were looking to lock down interest rates whenever they could.

But we saw the situation differently—that variable–interest rate loans would be the path to take—largely because of the lessons I was learning from history, particularly what happened to the US economy in the 1920s and 1930s when similar residential and commercial real estate bubbles burst. By studying that time period and understanding what similar things might happen again in our time, we began to develop the courage we needed to go against the grain and take meaningful action on the slew of opportunities we saw developing all around us.

I felt that there was a tremendous amount to be learned from studying how the government responded to the crisis—particularly what the Federal Reserve did—and in seeing how interest rates reacted to deficit spending. We saw the Obama administration responding in a way that seemed as if it were using a page out of FDR's playbook, both in terms of initiating a stimulus program as well as increasing regulation on Wall Street, which gave me confidence that we could see how things would unfold.

But what we didn't know was what would happen to capitalization rates (a valuation metric used to price different forms of real estate), which would be a key determinant in the price of real estate. What we were seeing was the pervasive pessimism that caused deal volume to drop by 90 percent because apartment owners didn't want to sell in what they believed to be a depressed environment for prices.

But that's also when I began to expand my research to include more modern theories on how our fiscal and monetary system works as a way to get further insight into how we might best take advantage of the Munger Moment staring back at us.

Chapter Ten

LESSONS FROM HISTORY

Mankind are so much the same, in all times and places, that
history informs us of nothing new or strange in this particular.
Its chief use is only to discover the constant and universal
principles of human nature.
—*David Hume*

The subprime lending boom that took place between 2003 and 2007 almost brought the global economy to its knees. Wall Street was available to feed and nurture a voracious demand for higher-yielding debt instruments sliced and diced into many different tranches via the securitization process. Most people understandably believed that this was a modern-day phenomenon. Although this contemporary form of securitization began in the late 1970s and had a remarkably successful run for nearly three decades until the financial alchemists on Wall Street created their own Frankenstein, the true origins go back to the 1920s.

Back then the retail-investing public was lured in to purchase real estate securities used to finance an urban construction boom, particularly in Chicago and New York City. Between 1922 and 1931, there were 235 buildings taller than two hundred feet constructed in New York. There has never been a ten-year period before or since that produced so many tall buildings. While this ultimately led to the creation of the beautiful skylines we see today in Chicago and New York City, it also left behind tremendous carnage among the gullible investing public.

In addition to the explosion of high-rise office buildings, there was also a tremendous boom in residential construction and values during this time. For example, between 1918 and 1926 it is estimated that the value of non-farm dwellings increased by more than 400 percent. Similar to Fannie Mae and Freddie Mac in the modern financial system, investors were attracted by "guaranteed mortgage participation certificates" (GMPCs), which were pools of mortgage cash flows issued by large title and insurance companies, who generally guaranteed their coupon at 5 percent. There was no implicit government guarantee as with Fannie and Freddie, but their track record and perceived financial strength made the investing public very comfortable with purchasing these securities. Demand was not only increased by the perceived guarantees but also by the powerful sales and distribution channels offered by bond houses to tap into public individuals' savings.

In 1936, after the virtual elimination of the real estate securities market and public disdain over the enormous corruption that was revealed (sound familiar?), Ernest Johnson did a comprehensive study of the public real estate securities market. The results show a boom of unprecedented scale. Between 1919 and 1931, total issuance exceeded $4.1 billion via 1,090 individual issues. Between 1919 and 1925, total yearly issuance grew from $57.7 million to $695.8 million, or an increase of nearly 1,106 percent. Buildings in New York and Chicago served as collateral for over 72 percent of securities with values in excess of $1 million. On the residential front, the total outstanding par value of GMPCs issued by the two largest guarantors, New York Title and Mortgage Company and Lawyer's Mortgage Company, grew from $187 million in 1917 to over $1.16 billion in 1931 (522 percent growth).

Like every other boom financed by unsophisticated investors with the capital allocated to increasingly more speculative ventures, this ended with a lot of capital being destroyed. An index created by Goetzmann and Newman to quantify the movement in price of real estate securities peaked in May 1928 at 100.10 and fell to a low of 24.75 in April 1933. Although by the end of 1935 some of the value was recouped, the securities still traded for less than fifty cents on the dollar.

The real estate boom spread to the stock market, which also collapsed in spectacular fashion when the market lost nearly 90 percent of its value between 1929 and 1932. The banking system essentially collapsed: deposits were lost, as they were not insured; economic activity contracted horrifically; and unemployment shot up to an estimated 25 percent. The combination of all of these factors and their similarities to what was happening in 2007 through 2009 convinced me that a good return on my time would be to study what was taking place during the Great Depression to see if it could help me answer the questions, What was going to happen to net operating incomes (NOI), and what was going to happen to the cost of capital?

My goal is to convey what we were thinking as events were unfolding and the decisions we were making in real time, rather than with the benefit of hindsight. Therefore, this section will also liberally use material that I wrote in the midst of the Great Recession. As I have mentioned before, I am drawn to very wise people whom history has proven to be prescient. Because there is very little new under the sun, we can obviously learn a lot from history, especially from people who demonstrated great judgment and foresight.

One of my personal historical mentors in this regard is Walter Lippmann, one of our country's great journalists. Lippmann died in 1974, but he was a prominent writer during World War I, the Great Depression, World War II, and the postwar, Cold War world. He was also very astute when it came to economic issues. He was an extraordinarily thoughtful person whose writings were clearly devoid of emotion: a welcome attribute given that he rarely shied away from controversial topics.

Is there anything we can learn from Lippmann about the United States' increasing reliance on foreign funding, the dollar, and much greater government involvement in the economy? I would assert that there is. I think the best economic model is the Great Depression and New Deal, so in the text that follows I will quote liberally from Lippmann articles written between 1932 and 1935.

There is a lot of concern being expressed by economists, politicians, investors, and, most importantly, the Chinese and Russians about the viability of the dollar as the world's reserve currency in light of unprecedented federal government deficits and borrowing. Many argue that we are at great risk, having to rely on foreigners (particularly foreign governments) to fund our deficits, and that when they lose confidence in the dollar and the security of US Treasury instruments they will sell or stop buying our debt, thereby sending interest rates through the roof. Lippmann wrote about this in 1934, and I think that what he had to say is very interesting in light of more recent events. Think China when you read *creditor* and the United States for *debtor*.

> The very fact that a country is a creditor, is owed more money than it owes, makes it very difficult for it to receive payments from foreigners. The only way around the difficulty is to reinvest the payments abroad, to lend back to the foreign debtor what he pays.
>
> That is what England did in the nineteenth century. It is what we did in the post-war years when the debts were being paid. But if you are a creditor country and won't lend back what you receive, then your choice is between not being paid on the one hand and doing less export business on the other.
>
> If we accept rubber and tin and whisky as payments in kind we shall sell less cotton, wheat, tobacco or automobiles. For

foreigners can buy from us only as much as they have dollars, plus whatever gold they have and what silver we will accept. And the amount of dollars they have with which to buy goods will depend upon how many dollars they receive when we buy goods and services from them, plus what we lend them. [1]

China and Russia (and now India as well) can talk about alternatives to the US dollar, or about not buying but rather selling US Treasuries, but I don't see this happening unless they want to significantly cut back on their exports to us. I do not think any of these nations would like to see this happen, particularly China, because of the social unrest that would ensue from the massive layoffs. China is already contending with a significant reduction in its exports and more layoffs, and I do not think it wants to see much more. My point is that it is in the world's best interest to manage an orderly rebalancing of the value of the dollar and world trade so that there is more consumption in China and less in the United States. A disorderly adjustment is in no one's best interest, and I think that the major economic players will make decisions based on what is in their interest rather than on what people think should happen or what is inevitable in their opinion. I think Walter Lippmann has it right, and he is the wise horse I am betting on as opposed to dollar bears who see the United States devolving into currency debasement and hyperinflation.

Conclusion: A large trade deficit will not lead to higher inflation and higher interest rates.

Lippmann's Assessment

Lippmann wrote an article that was published on December 30, 1934, just prior to President Roosevelt submitting his 1935 budget to Congress. In the article, Lippmann lays out the very real and legitimate debate

---

1. Walter Lippmann, Today and Tomorrow, *New York Herald Tribune*, June 16, 1934.

going on in the country between businessmen (who were worried about perpetual deficits and how this might lead to future inflation and a dollar collapse) and others (who were more concerned about the here and now and believed that those out of work should be taken care of). Allow me to quote liberally, as I think the debate that took place then is still very relevant to today:

> The question which will be before the country next week when the President submits his budget to Congress is a hard question. It involves the interrelated problems of relief ["welfare," in today's language], unemployment and 'business confidence,' which means the willingness of business executives to spend money and of bankers and investors to lend money for capital goods. On this question there has been raging a passionate conflict of opinion between those who fear inflation in the future and those who are horrified by the misery of the unemployed in the present. The dispute is generally presented as an argument between tough-minded realists on the one hand and tender-minded humanitarians on the other.

> The test of Mr. Roosevelt's statesmanship will be whether he can formulate and make intelligible to the public a program that gives confidence equally to business executives and to the unemployed. There will be some who say that it is impossible to do this. But to say that is to declare that there is an irreconcilable antagonism within the existing social order and in a spirit of defeatism to accept the premises of the doctrines of class war.

> The case of the realists is that a series of large government deficits which have no visible end must lead to the destruction of the currency. As that would mean the destruction

of savings, middle class incomes and real wages, it would be social catastrophe of the first order. It is no answer to this argument to show that our nation's debt, per capita or in terms of national income, is very much smaller than that of Great Britain [think Japan today]. For the argument of the realists is that if business men and investors see no end to the deficits, their willingness to invest will be paralyzed; if they do not invest, the unemployed will not be re-employed; if unemployment continues, relief continues, deficits will continue.

Thus a vicious circle will be set up from which they see no escape except through a destruction of the currency and a general collapse.

No realistic estimate of the possibilities of recovery in the near future can promise that more than half the unemployed will find jobs in private industry. For given a great revival of confidence in America there will still remain a large residue of unemployment due to the less of foreign trade and unless miracles happen all over the world, that foreign trade will not quickly be restored.

It is only prudent, therefore, to assume that there will be an abnormally large number of unemployed for some time to come. The realists say that the best policy is to feed them as cheaply as possible and then to let them wait for full recovery. Is this a truly realistic policy? Let us pass over the social dangers, the deterioration of men in idleness, the effect on their children or being brought up in a household supported by a dole, the recruiting of these men for lawless or revolutionary movements. Let us ignore the lessons of experience, past and contemporary, as to the peril to a state when it has within it a large mass of able-bodied, disinherited men.

Lippmann ends up siding with the camp that believes the deficit is a long-term issue, far superseded by the problems of the day. He asks,

> What good will it do us to balance the Federal budget if that involves a policy which keeps the national economy unbalanced? Balanced budgets are highly desirable. But they existed in the pre-depression years. And they did not save us. Why? Because the economic system was out of balance at several different points and this imbalance finally destroyed the budgetary balance in all the leading countries.[2]

In an even more fascinating article published on January 9, 1935, after Roosevelt's budget was submitted to Congress, Lippmann summarizes the key principles that he believed were underlying the expenditure decisions. What comes through loud and clear is that the way out of the deficit was through economic growth, and that this was no time to stop federal spending because of the huge number of unemployed Americans. Once again, I think this has tremendous relevance today. I have not studied the Obama administration's policies with the degree of depth that would allow me to assess what its core principles are, but, on the other hand, I felt that President Obama had been taking pages out of the FDR playbook since entering office. So I am willing to give him the benefit of the doubt that he subscribes to the principles laid out by Lippmann when I drill down more deeply into his speeches and policies. Lippmann writes:

> The heart of the matter is to be found in a passage in the budget message where the President says:

2. Walter Lippmann, Today and Tomorrow, *New York Herald Tribune*, Dec. 20, 1934.

I am . . . submitting to the congress a budget . . . which balances except for expenditures to give work to the unemployed . . . such deficits as occurs will be due solely to this cause, and it may be expected to decline as rapidly as private industry is able to re-employ those who are now out of work.

Underlying this statement, which must be read, of course, in conjunction with the message, are certain implied basic principles which it may be useful to list:

1. It is the duty of the government to provide the unemployed with the opportunity to work. That is to say, there is a right to work.

2. This right is not a substitute for private employment. It is a supplement to it, when private employment is lacking. Therefore, the public work should be non-competitive with private enterprise; the wages paid on it should be fixed at a point which is above what men must have to live but below the ordinary wages of private employment.

3. The supplementary public work should be paid for not out of taxes but out of borrowing. For when private industry is not employing the unemployed and is not drawing upon idle capital, the government can safely (and should) as a matter of policy, use capital that would otherwise be idle.

4. As private industry absorbs the unemployed, public work should diminish. As private industry draws upon the capital market, government borrowing should diminish. Thus the

budget should come into balance when private industry is in balance.

5. Since the balancing of the budget is made dependent upon the revival of business, it becomes the duty of the government to reject policies which obstruct revival and to adopt policies which promote it. This involves a refusal to raise the costs of production before profits are earned, and therefore a refusal to encourage monopolistic prices, monopolistic wages, and the monopolistic restriction of output. That means drastic revision of NRA and serious reconsideration of many aspects of the AAA. It involves an administration and interpretation of the securities act which will not merely stop abuses but will positively promote refunding and new financing. It involves the abandonment of merely punitive and terroristic attacks on private business and banking in favor of direct regulation of specific evils.

6. Since the policy calls for a deliberate use of government expenditure to put unemployed labor and capital to work, its execution requires unified executive initiative and control in the realms of expenditure, taxation, and borrowing. Therefore, it is necessary to resist all proposals to disorganize the policy by prepayment of the bonus, the Townsend plan, printing of greenbacks, and the like.[3]

Hindsight proved that devaluing the dollar and large government involvement in getting people back to work (although not as successful as the Roosevelt administration would have liked) did generate extraordinary economic growth between 1933 and 1937. It was only when the

---

3. Walter Lippmann, Today and Tomorrow, *New York Herald Tribune*, Jan. 9 1935.

Federal Reserve got very nervous about all the excess reserves in the banking system and began tightening credit and Roosevelt focused on cutting the deficit that the economic recovery was stopped in its tracks. I do not see the Fed repeating the same mistake or spending being cut, and, therefore, we will see continued Federal Reserve involvement in the financial markets and short-term interest rates remaining low for the foreseeable future. I am also in the Walter Lippmann camp that the best cure for our deficit is greater economic growth, and I do not see this occurring without government involvement in getting more people back to work.

Therefore, we will continue to see large deficits and an orderly decline of the US dollar, because this will help our export sectors, although it will be accompanied by periodic, nervous statements by investors and foreign governments about the US embarking on a reckless path of dollar devaluation, socialism, and hyperinflation.

Whether these beliefs will turn out to be wise or not, only time will tell. One can never know if economic growth would have been stronger and more durable without such large deficits and government spending. On the other hand, we should have objective evidence as to whether our country will have suffered from painful bouts of inflation and whether the dollar depreciated in a way that caused us long-term economic harm. Although inflation is beneficial for real estate, I believe we will all be more prosperous if it is held in check in a way that results in more people being employed. This too, is good for real estate and is the scenario that I am betting on, despite being in the distinct minority.

* * *

Post-script: This turned out to be quite accurate, as the budget deficit has come down considerably and inflation has remained very tame; all the while interest rates remained at historically low levels.

Chapter Eleven

FINDING THE RIGHT CAP RATE

In mathematics the art of proposing a question
must be held of higher value than solving it.
—George Cantor

I was driving with my daughter one day when I blurted out, "MAD!" She was a little surprised, but she went along with it and asked what I was mad about. I said, "No, I'm not mad about anything, MAD stands for something." She said, "Money and death?" I laughed knowing that she was more onto something than she realized, given everything going on in the world.

I told her it stands for Mutually Assured Destruction. Even though she was twelve at the time, she had a fascination with the Cold War, so I was happy to explain it to her, especially since I was a political science major. MAD was a defense doctrine assuring that both the Soviets and Americans would be wiped out in any nuclear war they started. This assurance resulted from the belief that the country being attacked would respond with massive force. The key to this doctrine was having the weaponry and the other side believing that you would use it when attacked.

In the context of MAD, assurance results in a negative outcome—mutual destruction. There are forms of positive assurance, however, and this is what our financial markets had been lacking and why the Treasury and global central banks took extraordinary steps to provide liquidity and deposit insurance in the wake of the 2008 financial crisis. (It is somewhat ironic that the assurance provided by private parties from 2003 to 2007 enjoyed the trust of investors when they should not have had such confidence, while today many don't seem to trust the government assurance.)

The bull market in *complexity* had crashed. The rocket scientists recruited to our investment banks, rating agencies, and hedge funds unleashed a monster of complexity in which incomprehensible financial and statistical models replaced common sense. Our esteemed rating agencies assigned AAA ratings to financial instruments that should never have had such a stamp of approval. A profusion of hedging instruments gave investors the illusion that they had no downside if a bond defaulted, because they had purchased insurance against such an event. This confidence led to investors wanting to invest in more of the risky bonds—because, after all, they were covered by insurance. In turn, this led to an explosion in the issuance of low-quality bonds that were dramatically mispriced (their interest rates were too low), because investors believed they could insure against the risk of these bonds defaulting. It is analogous to building in a flood zone on the basis that you can get insurance.

When the Safety Net Is Ripped

Unfortunately, the risk no one analyzed very accurately was that those companies writing the insurance were not as strong as they thought, particularly since financial problems tend to cascade and take many players down at the same time. Thus, at the very time you need the insurance the most, it is at the greatest risk of not being there. The insurance companies writing the "financial flood insurance" became insolvent, and the policyholders had only the federal government to look to.

Investors who sold insurance to protect bondholders of Lehman Brothers against default had a rude awakening when they had to shell out nearly $400 billion to make the insurance buyers whole. The system could not take too many Lehman Brothers–type events, so lenders began hoarding cash to cover such unanticipated events in the future, as well as to cover other financial commitments made during the boom times. Banks were seeing an outflow of deposits to Treasuries at precisely the most inopportune time. They refused to lend to each other. Everyone seemed to be lacking assurance.

While assurance in the Cold War promised mutual destruction of the Soviets and Americans, now a lack of assurance threatened destruction of the global financial system. The Federal Reserve knew this, and therefore it expanded its balance sheet to provide liquidity to banks at an unprecedented rate, as the following chart shows.

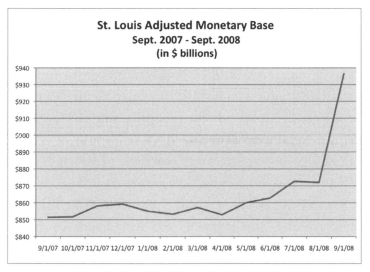

Source: St. Louis Federal Reserve Bank (data in billions)

With mistrust and fear permeating the psyche of savers and investors around the world, the governmental authorities and central banks of the leading industrialized countries tried to ameliorate this situation. They did this by guaranteeing banking deposits and money market funds, by injecting capital into banks, by purchasing commercial paper, and by lending money to banks and taking back collateral of a very questionable quality. They injected a flood of money into the system. Despite all of these actions, people still fled from risky, non-guaranteed investments to the safety and security of fully guaranteed Treasuries. If this is what people wanted, then this is what the government would give them.

The Treasury would offer assurance to global investors, and these investors would part with their capital at a very low return. The Treasury would exploit this fearful state and would use this low-cost capital to unclog the banking system by injecting liquidity into banks and buying their unmarketable mortgage securities at attractive prices. They would inventory these assets and would deliver them to the marketplace when fear had dissipated and the inevitable greed manifested itself again.

I know, I know; what about inflation? Forget it. Inflation is dead; debt bubbles do not unwind with inflation. Japan flooded its system with money for fifteen years, and there was no inflation to speak of there. People worry about the rapid increase in money supply, but this is a very different worry when collateral values are collapsing and the net worth of our highly leveraged financial intermediaries is shrinking.

For those who are not students of economic history, it may come as a surprise that the actions taken by the Treasury via its $700 billion rescue package were almost exactly out of the playbook of the Reconstruction Finance Corporation (RFC) created by Herbert Hoover and kicked into high gear by President Roosevelt in 1933. The Bush and Obama administrations didn't want to say this for fear of scaring people by linking the more recent meltdown to the conditions present during the Great Depression, thereby tying themselves to New Deal–type actions.

People worried about inflation and government deficits during the 1930s, too. This fear proved to be misplaced, because between 1934 and

1947 short-term Treasury bills never yielded more than 1 percent. As of this writing, they yield 0.02 percent: the lowest yield since 1941. The following is from a speech given by Jesse Jones, the head of the RFC in October 1934, as printed in the *New York Times*.

Greatest Single Asset Is Seen in Real Estate

Our plan to assist the mortgage situation was announced on Sept. 27, with the hearty endorsement of President Roosevelt. The news release, which he approved, stated that our nation's greatest single asset is real estate, and that because a few big centres were overbuilt and many of the buildings improvidently financed, was no reason why real estate or real estate securities should be forever condemned.

Real estate, in some form, constitutes the savings and investments of a very large percentage of our citizenship and these investments should be preserved as far as it is possible to preserve them, without loss to the government.

The release also stated that the purposes desired are:

First—To provide mortgage money for new construction with a view to increasing employment and stimulating structural material markets.

Second—To enable distressed owners of mortgages, whether whole mortgages, split mortgages or mortgage certificates, to borrow reasonably upon these mortgages at fair interest rates and not to be forced to sell at sacrifice prices.

Third—To enable borrowers to refinance mortgages where the value and/or income of the mortgaged property, and the ability of the borrower to meet interest and principal payments, will support the mortgage.

Fourth—To assist in the preservation and reorganization of distressed properties for the protection of mortgage bonds or certificates, including second mortgages and equities, where the holder has a real chance of saving his property, the primary purpose being to re-establish by private capital and private initiative a sound mortgage market throughout the country, with the assistance and cooperation of the RFC.

This movement supplements the Federal Housing Administration, whose activities should have the hearty support of every bank in the United States. It also supplements the work of the Home Owners Loan Corporation and the Farm Credit Administration. It is intended to establish sound, properly managed mortgage banks to complement these, as well as life insurance companies, building and loan associations, saving banks and others doing a mortgage business, with a view to making available mortgage money at fair rates and on a sound basis for all legitimate purposes.

It is a big task finding work for the unemployed and the banker can help more than any other class. It is the responsibility of the banks, business and industry to mold and distribute the products of agriculture and labor for the use of all and in a way that every one may have a share.

It will be through cooperation and without too much pride of authorship or ideas, all pulling in the same direction under the leadership of Franklin Roosevelt, that we will solve our problems.

In closing I would remind you—lest we forget—that the entire banking situation was saved by the constructive policies of the Roosevelt Administration. If it had not been for those policies, made effective largely through the RFC, with the cooperation of the Treasury, the Controller of the Currency and State banking authorities, many banks that are now strong and sound, would have been in the discard and the others would have had a hard time maintaining their existence.

As in the most recent crisis, real estate was the crux of the problem back then, and the government was looking at ways of creating more liquidity for banks that were saddled by problem loans while also encouraging them to work out loans and lend to new borrowers. This was done by investing in preferred stock of many of the banking institutions and by buying difficult-to-market mortgage assets. I think you will be surprised by how today's situation parallels some of the challenges faced in the 1930s.

By the time Roosevelt had come into office, industrial production had dropped by more than 50 percent but was finally on the upswing, although it did experience some violent downdrafts over the next year or so. It took seven years for it to reach its 1929 peak. Surprising to most people, however, is the fact that it reached a new peak in May 1937 only to drop by approximately 33 percent over the next twelve months. Those were some very wild times. More recently, on the other hand, industrial production peaked in January 2008 and then dropped by a far smaller amount. The unemployment rate reached nothing like the 25 percent rate during the Great Depression.

One measurement of stress in the system is the difference in yield between riskier securities (BAA corporate bonds) and less risky ones (AAA corporate bonds) expressed as a ratio. When there is very little fear, investors are willing to accept similar returns from the more risky bonds to those for the less risky ones. The opposite is true when fear dominates greed. The following charts show this ratio; the first shows from 1919 through 1950 (Great Depression and World War II) and the second covers 1951 through October 2008. The first chart shows that this ratio reached extremes never seen in the second chart. With the exception of a brief period in 1958, the year 2008 was the most fearful time since the Great Depression and World War II.

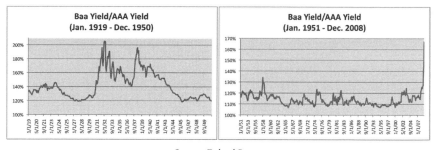

Source: Federal Reserve

One of the interesting takeaways from these charts is that during the four periods of extremes in this ratio (January 1958, February 1975, November 1982, and October 2002) the stock market hit bottom within one to five months, each and every time. The obvious question for me in 2008 was, when would this ratio peak? With the stock market down nearly 40 percent, pessimism at record levels, and global governments and central banks willing to throw in whatever capital was needed to resuscitate the patient, I thought we were much closer to a bottom. I also recognized that it was very rare for a bear market to close lower than previous bear market lows. To reach the previous bear market low of October 2002, the S&P 500 would have to have fallen another 15 percent. Finally, the largest drop in after-tax corporate profits in the previous sixty years had been 28 percent, between 1979 and 1982. Thus, in the absence of a meaningful contraction in price-earnings multiples, the 40 percent drop in the market should have been sufficiently discounting a drop in corporate profits. With the economic statistics set to get worse, the federal government's deficit about to explode, housing prices likely continuing to drop, and the job market on course to remain very weak, the question on my mind was, How much of this had been factored into the prices for debt and equity? I asserted that much of it had, otherwise I feared that MAD would really take over.

From a CWS perspective, we decided to ensure that all of our properties were well capitalized to weather the storm and to take advantage of the almost assured (there's a derivative of that word "assurance") curtailment of apartment construction and favorable demand fundamentals. We would do this by raising additional funds from investors where we believed it was necessary and by being more aggressive about raising acquisition capital so that we would have a loaded gun, ready to fire when the inevitable opportunities (i.e., overleveraged property owners needing to sell or refinance) presented themselves. Ron Witten, a leading apartment researcher and a former speaker at one of our annual meetings, adopted the mantra "Heaven in 2011" for apartments, based on his belief that demand would significantly exceed supply and rents would rise rapidly. Some might have called us MAD, but we believed that the worst was actually behind us.

During the depths of the Great Recession in 2008 and 2009 it was nearly impossible to determine what the right valuation metric was for apartment investments. Fear was pervasive, people didn't know if net operating income (NOI) was going to fall off a cliff, lenders were very conservative, and there was a perception that the market would be flooded with properties being sold by distressed sellers. In addition, the valuation of publicly traded real estate investment trusts (REITs) and their preferreds were at extraordinary yields. These are just the environments I find invigorating and challenging.

Learning from the Past, Not Repeating It

With fear being so pervasive, my natural instinct was to determine if it was time to be greedy. I knew that single-family housing was not going to lead us out of the recession, because it got us into recession. And there was no way the government would support this sector as it had in the past. The contraction in credit was not only going to dramatically reduce the supply of new single-family homes, but it would also have a very large impact on apartments as well. Eventually, when the economy did recover, new households would form, and nearly all of those would have to rent because of the home lenders' much tighter requirements. In addition, renting provides tremendous flexibility to allow people to go to where the jobs are, because they are not tied down to an illiquid, high–transaction cost asset like a single-family home.

Finally, after having dabbled in the high-yield investing market in 1990 and 2002, I knew that the extraordinary spreads being offered in lower-rated debt constituted a once-in-a-lifetime investment opportunity that would be very fleeting. The cost of capital would not remain that high for too long, apartments would be the first asset class to recover, and the continued (prudent) lending by Fannie Mae and Freddie Mac in the apartment sector would help stabilize values. So what was the right value? I turned to the 1930s (yet again) for some guidance. I looked for any kind of information that would give me some guidance in terms of what cap rates were at the bottom of the Great Depression in the 1930s. After searching high and low, I found the mother lode with an article from July 1, 1938 in the *New York Times*.

What is so great about this article is that it covers four years; there is no dispute regarding the NOI—only the cap rates to be used. Naturally, the owner wanted a higher cap rate (lower valuation) and the taxing authority wanted a lower one (higher valuation). Regardless, however, the range was a low of 5 percent for the taxing authority and 6 percent for the owner: pretty much the same cap rates that we felt properties should be trading for in a more normal environment, especially given that we thought that we would be in a low

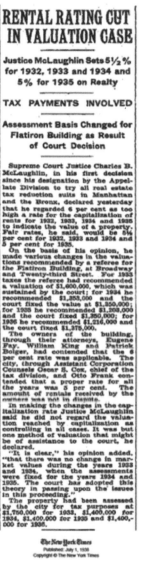

RENTAL RATING CUT IN VALUATION CASE

Justice McLaughlin Sets 5½ % for 1932, 1933 and 1934 and 5% for 1935 on Realty

TAX PAYMENTS INVOLVED

Assessment Basis Changed for Flatiron Building as Result of Court Decision

Supreme Court Justice Charles B. McLaughlin, in his first decision since his designation by the Appellate Division to try all real estate tax reduction suits in Manhattan and the Bronx, declared yesterday that he regarded 6 per cent as too high a rate for the capitalization of rents for 1932, 1933, 1934 and 1935 to indicate the value of a property. Fair rates, he said, would be 5½ per cent for 1932, 1933 and 1934 and 5 per cent for 1935.

On the basis of his opinion, he made various changes in the valuations recommended by a referee for the Flatiron Building, at Broadway and Twenty-third Street. For 1933 taxes the referee had recommended a valuation of $1,600,000, which was sustained by the court; for 1934 he recommended $1,253,000 and the court fixed the value at $1,350,000; for 1935 he recommended $1,203,000 and the court fixed $1,350,000; for 1936 he recommended $1,216,000 and the court fixed $1,375,000.

The owners of the building, through their attorneys, Eugene Fay, William King and Patrick Bolger, had contended that the 6 per cent rate was applicable. The city, through Assistant Corporation Counsels Oscar S. Cox, chief of the tax division, and Otto Frank contended that a proper rate for all the years was 5 per cent. The amount of rentals received by the owners was not in dispute.

In making the changes in the capitalization rate Justice McLaughlin said he did not regard the valuation reached by capitalization as controlling in all cases. It was but one method of valuation that might be of assistance to the court, he declared.

"It is clear," his opinion added, "that there was no change in market values during the years 1933 and 1934, when the assessments were fixed for the years 1934 and 1935. The court has adopted this theory in passing upon the issues in this proceeding."

The property had been assessed by the city for tax purposes at $1,750,000 for 1933, $1,400,000 for 1934, $1,400,000 for 1935 and $1,400,000 for 1936.

The New York Times
Published: July 1, 1938
Copyright © The New York Times

interest rate environment for a while. Here was some fairly strong evidence that during the worst economic period in the twentieth century—with unemployment approaching 25 percent and widespread vacancies in commercial real estate and apartments—cap rates were in the 5 to 6 percent range.

At almost every bottom it feels like things are either getting worse or, at best, not getting better; it is hard to find a catalyst for recovery. The post–financial crisis "Great Recession" of recent years was no different. Yet, once financial markets began to stabilize and the cost and availability of credit began to improve for corporations, we believed that we would be entering the sweet spot for apartment investing.

Chapter Twelve

MODERN MONETARY THEORY

*Thus, the task is not so much to see what no one
yet has seen, but to think what nobody yet has thought
about that which everybody sees.*
—*Arthur Schopenhauer*

In previous chapters I showed how the political and cultural landscape had changed to allow for much more aggressive intervention to create jobs at the expense of people's concerns about deficits, inflation, and the dollar. The parallels gave me confidence that recovery would take hold and that the main analytical emphasis should be on interest and cap rates since the supply-demand relationship for apartments looked quite favorable. We saw a combination of dramatically reduced supply, soon-to-be-improving demand fundamentals, positive demographics, banks with no interest or capacity to make construction loans, and rents far too low to justify building new apartments. To us, these factors appeared to be coalescing in a very favorable way for apartment owners. Financing became much more conservative, with Freddie Mac and Fannie Mae being the only viable lenders. The increasingly focused lending to only substantial firms with strong track records could only be positive for CWS.

The initial focus of this chapter highlights the thinking of Marriner Eccles, the Federal Reserve chairman from November 1934 through July 1951, and how applicable that was to what Federal Reserve chairman Ben Bernanke was contending with during the depths of the Great Recession. This analysis attempts to create some insight into what would happen to interest rates in the future as we were determining the right prices to pay for properties and how we should finance the properties in our portfolio, including new acquisitions. Finally, it was critical to understand the differences between then and now and to see if there were modern-day thinkers to whom I could turn to make sure we were correctly analyzing where we were and where we were headed in the context of today's modern monetary system.

We were in unusual times between 2008 and 2010 (and still are to an extent today) with the Fed "printing" trillions of dollars and the government spending all those stimulus dollars. It was valid to be worried about what this would do to inflation and interest rates. After all, logic would suggest that we'd have to see rates go higher as we were accumulating all of this debt, and the scale of the deficit was simply beyond human comprehension.

How could we ever hope to repay the accumulated debt? Why would people like the Chinese and other foreigners continue to buy our debt when they saw us debasing our currency through all the spending and money printing? It was an important question for me to ponder dispassionately, but there was so much political and ideological noise. One way of answering this question was to first go back to the 1920s and 1930s and then overlay some more modern thinking to help generate an understanding of the government's reaction function and the monetary system.

The reaction functions in the 1930s were very similar to what took place during the Great Recession. Spending increased significantly, the banking system was bailed out, and the Federal Reserve was loose in its monetary policy (until 1937) and kept interest rates low for many years. Similarities of thinking existed among Marriner Eccles (the Federal

Reserve chairman during the Depression years), Ben Bernanke (a student of the Great Depression), and now Janet Yellen. After reading a number of Eccles's speeches, I came to realize how close Bernanke's thinking was to his. The difference is that Eccles was much more blunt about his views, which had changed dramatically since he took over as chairman of the Fed, as opposed to Bernanke, who seemed to be trying to navigate through turbulent political and social waters. Bernanke knew that what needed to be done to bail out the banks and provide large fiscal stimuli was not always tasteful, so he had to tread lightly.

Eccles was a private sector businessman from Utah who was a millionaire by age twenty-two. He was also a very successful banker. During the Great Depression he lent his skills and knowledge to the government by helping to create the Emergency Banking Act of 1933 and the Federal Deposit Insurance Corporation. As the magnitude of the crisis became more and more apparent, Eccles's views started to evolve and change. I will cite a few powerful excerpts of speeches he gave that helped convince me not only that the government would have to take a very powerful and active role in helping us to get out of the Great Recession, but that the Fed would have to step in much more aggressively to be the buyer of last resort and would keep rates down for a very long period of time.

Eccles shifted from a free market fundamentalist to one who realized that the government had an important, stabilizing role in the economy. The massive collapse in industrial production, GDP, and employment in a few short years made him question everything he had previously believed. From my perspective, Eccles has the best definition of what "sound money" should be. He said in a radio speech on June 4, 1935:

> We have sound money when our system behaves in such a way as to help rather than hinder the full and efficient use of our productive resources. We have sound money when the energy and skill of American workers, the productive capacity of our great industrial plant and equipment, and

the fruitfulness of our land and natural resources are used in such a way as to make our real income of goods and services as large as possible, not merely for a few prosperous years followed by a period of idleness and want, but for year after year of enduring stability. This, it seems to me, should be the criterion of the soundness of money, and not the amount of gold that is stored in the vaults of the Treasury.

Eccles also expressed some strong views against the idealistic, Hooverian notion that through traditional American thrift and hard work we can pull ourselves out of the Depression. This is how he debunked the notion that we only need to rely on the private sector without needing government involvement:

> The theory of hard work and thrift as a means of pulling us out of the depression is unsound economically. True hard work means more production but thrift and economy mean less consumption. Now reconcile those two forces, will you? . . . There is only one agency . . . that can turn the cycle upward and that is the government. The government . . . must so regulate . . . the economic structure as to give men who are able, willing, and worthy to work the opportunity to work, and to guarantee to them sustenance for their families and protection against want and destitution.

Part of the problem why the private sector could not be relied upon to get us out of the problem was due to over-saving:

> It now appears that, when surplus funds are saved or accumulated, whether by corporations or individuals, they go into the capital market and provide more facilities and produce more goods and provide more transportation than the

people as a whole are able to buy; in other words, creating a situation where productive capacity gets out of balance with consumer buying-power, so that we have the paradoxical situation of an economy of abundance with millions of people out of work and idle factories and unused goods as the flow of money stops and slows up.

Finally, for those who were outraged by the bailout of Bear Stearns, AIG, Merrill Lynch, Fannie Mae, Freddie Mac, and others, this is what Eccles had to say in terms of why such actions need to be done during times of extreme financial dislocation:

Thus the emphasis would be taken off the variable yardstick of fluctuating market values and put where it belongs: on true worth, measured over a longer period and by broader experience. At a time when the normal security and money markets are demoralized, the Reserve System is the only means whereby liquidity can be provided, because it can convert sound but temporarily unmarketable assets into money.[1]

I am struck by the parallels to what we were contending with during the Great Recession. Although I now see how Eccles analyzed the situation and responded, there were differences in how the monetary system was organized then versus now. The most important is that we are no longer on a fixed exchange rate regime. Today, the US dollar floats against most of the currencies of the world. I wanted to make sure that I understood to the best of my abilities how our system truly worked to make sure that I didn't automatically assume that, despite the parallels and similar policy responses in the 1930s, the system would respond in

---

1. Board of Governors of the Federal Reserve System, Eccles, Marriner S., and Federal Reserve Board, *Statements and Speeches of Marriner S. Eccles*, 1934–1951, https://fraser.stlouisfed.org /title/?id=446.

the same way if it had changed in meaningful ways. It was now time to turn to some modern-day wise men. These turned out to be Richard Koo and Warren Mosler (and a number of his disciples).

A lightbulb went off after reading Richard Koo's *Balance Sheet Recession*. It led me to realize that large deficits were nothing to fear in the midst of the Great Recession, but they were absolutely necessary in the face of massive deleveraging by households as a result of the housing crash and rapidly increasing unemployment. Koo utilized the sectoral balances approach created by Wayne Godley—a methodology that proves that investments and savings must equal each other in any economy.

There are four major sectors of the economy: households, businesses, government, and trade. Typically businesses and government are in deficit while households save, and trade is in deficit. During the housing boom, some of the traditional roles reversed. Households (the traditional savers) went into deficit, while corporations (the traditional spenders) began saving substantially. With corporations continuing to save, capital coming into the country via the capital account surplus, and households now needing to save due to the collapse of their largest asset (their homes), this left only one entity that could spend if the economy was to avoid a deflationary collapse. That entity was the federal government, especially since state governments were cutting back spending, along with households.

One of the important realizations that I came away with after reading Richard Koo's *Balance Sheet Recession* is that the only way to avoid a deflationary collapse in the economy was for the federal government to step in very aggressively and bring spending to the table when so many other parts of the economy were in a savings mode. And while some found this ideologically distasteful, it was important for me to begin to evaluate it in a dispassionate manner. I've found that ideology is an investor's biggest enemy, since it brings bias and inflexibility to the table at times when open-mindedness, flexibility, and creativity are needed to try and figure out what is going on.

Having realized that we were going to have trillion-dollar deficits as far as the eye could see, I then had the following questions to contend with for our business:

- Would this be good for the economy, and would it create an economic floor that would allow businesses to hire people?
- As people were hired, would new households be formed, and would they become renter households because the single-family home market was in such disarray?

Assuming the answers were yes, the name of the game would be renting, since that would allow for people to build their savings and their creditworthiness. It would allow them to have mobility and flexibility, not being tied down to an illiquid, expensive asset such that they couldn't move to where the new jobs were.

But from our standpoint, it was important for us to be able to keep answering the two most important questions that were easy to ask but not so easy to answer:

1. What's going to happen to my net operating income?

2. What's going to happen to my cost of capital?

The answers to my earlier questions led me to believe that the net operating income had a healthy future once the economy started to recover. New apartment construction was at fifty-year lows, and there was not going to be new development for a while. The demand fundamentals clearly favored apartments. And as previously discussed in the cap rates section, there was some historical precedent for cap rates being in the 5 to 6 percent range, despite many investors thinking they should be much higher due to the tremendous amount of uncertainty prevalent in the economy. This belief was also predicated on interest rates not rising. This was clearly a minority view, given the concerns that all of the federal spending and monetary stimulus would inevitably lead to inflation. But would it?

I can't overstate how important it was to get this right, because if one were fearful about rates rising, then one would be more conservative in the bids one would make to purchase properties, despite being bullish about NOI prospects. In addition, it would also influence borrowers to lock in longer-term, fixed-rate loans to take interest-rate risk off the table.

On the other hand, if one felt that rates would not only stay stable but also have a reasonable likelihood of dropping, then one could bid more aggressively for properties and utilize variable-rate financing to take advantage of the stable-to-declining rates; variable-rate loans are typically 1 to 2 percent lower at origination versus the prevailing fixed-rate loans. If this advantage not only remains in place but widens as rates drop, then this can generate significantly higher returns for leveraged investors, since a 1 to 2 percent per year difference can translate to 2 to 5 percent per year higher equity returns, depending on the leverage.

I often joke that I have three kids: Jacob, Ariella, and LIBOR (the London Interbank Offered Rate, a widely used benchmark for interest rates). I have been fascinated by the history of interest rates for a very long time, because it is such a critical part of generating excess returns or avoiding underperformance for real estate investors. The reflexive reaction of industry participants to only using fixed-rate debt has often produced returns quite a bit less than those willing to expose themselves to interest-rate risk via variable-rate loans. My research has shown that investors would have been far better off being variable over the last thirty years or so versus fixed, and that most people end up paying too much of an insurance premium for taking interest-rate risk off the table. They unknowingly have increased operational risk, because the higher debt service results in the requirement to have a higher level of revenue to break even. There is no free lunch.

I don't remember how, exactly, but after reading Koo's *Balance Sheet*

Recession I stumbled upon "Modern Monetary Theory" (MMT). It is an out-of-the-mainstream philosophy (or viewpoint, or theory) that explains how the monetary system works in today's modern, digital age. A few blogs and a couple of ebooks helped me get my arms around principles of Modern Monetary Theory, including *Pragmatic Capitalism*, *Mike Norman Economics*, *Mosler Economics*, and (to a lesser extent) *The Big Picture Blog* and *Naked Capitalism*. Warren Mosler is really the father of MMT—a brilliant, iconoclastic individual, a very successful investor, and author of two very important books: *Seven Deadly Innocent Frauds* and *Soft Currency Economics* (both of which I recommend).

As I began to research MMT, I started to think, "Wow, this has all the answers!" Yet there was so much hostility and anger from monetarists, Austrians, and free market fundamentalists about what the Federal Reserve was doing (versus what MMT said was needed). MMT predicates itself on the belief that once you have a fiat currency—a currency backed by absolutely nothing and supplied by a treasury or government that has a monopoly control over that currency—there is no obligation for it to be converted into another currency or commodity. That currency has value, because taxes (which are required to legally live in the society) have to be paid in that currency. Therefore the currency will always have value, and it can be used as a medium of exchange, because people will always need to get that currency to pay their taxes.

It is important to note that in this modern age, where spending is really managed by keystrokes on computers and is reduced to a string of electronic ones and zeros moving around the world, there's very little physical money actually circulating. So when the government writes a check to pay its workers or suppliers, it does not need to borrow or raise money from taxes in order to spend. It is hard for people to understand how money can be created apparently out of thin air, so they worry unnecessarily about, "Oh my gosh, how are we going to be able to fund this deficit?"

The reason why Treasury bonds and bills exist is essentially to give owners of those securities the ability to earn more interest by holding them for longer periods of time. The Treasury determines how much money it is going to raise in an offering not by how much it really needs to run the government, but by what it considers to be the right amount of reserves to have in the banking system. And it can clear those excess reserves by issuing Treasury securities.

So, basically, banks can take money that's sitting there earning barely more than zero percent interest (and is accessible at any time) and they can exchange those reserves for longer-term, guaranteed instruments at 2 or 3 percent for ten years. Treasury securities give them many options to choose from in order to meet their needs. So once again, it is more about reserve management than it is about the government needing taxes or borrowing to fund itself. It just enters keystrokes on the computer.

So what are taxes for, then, if not to fund the government? There are two major reasons for taxes:

1. To control inflation. If the economy is too hot, then taxation can be used to withdraw buying power from the economy.

2. To control savings (i.e., capital that is not being circulated). Tax policy can be utilized to discourage savings and encourage direct spending in areas of the economy that have a social good. I'm not here to comment on what's good or bad; just to explain the philosophy behind MMT.

Dread the Fed

From our business point of view, it is important to know what this means for interest rates. Let's look at an analogy from Cullen Roche, the proprietor of Pragcap.com (Pragmatic Capitalism): "Imagine a dog on a leash. It can call the shots for a while if it wants to (and if the owner lets it). But if it strays too far, or gets too out of control, the owner can simply yank the leash and stop the dog dead in its tracks. And that's the Federal Reserve."

The Federal Reserve has absolute control over short-term interest rates. In fact, if the Fed did not intervene, then the excess reserves in the economy or in the banking system would be such that they would continuously be lent out at a short-term rate approaching zero. It's somewhat complicated to explain why, but that's what would happen. So the Fed intervenes (based on its policy objectives) to make short-term interest rates nonzero. I will expand on this in the chapter "Go Variable, Young Man."

For longer-term interest rates, this is where the leash analogy really comes in. Suppose the Fed has certain policy objectives to keep stable inflation in the context of full employment. It can use its bully pulpit to tell the market, "Look, this is where we want rates to be. You can go ahead and buy bonds and at higher yields, but we've got a pretty powerful tool (our money printing presses) to buy unlimited quantities of these bonds. So don't get too cocky, because we can move rates either lower or higher, or we can sell all these securities."

In a nutshell, the Fed can take action or merely threaten to take action based on its vastly superior buying power.

Putting all that together, I came to the conclusion that there was going to be no material movement in rates—particularly on a short-term basis. In fact, the Fed came out and said that they probably wouldn't move until unemployment is at 6.5 percent or below and the inflation rate is at 2.5 percent or below, and my own analysis convinced me that this wouldn't happen for a while.

While everyone was fearful of interest rates going higher and desperate to fix at a lower rate for the long term, I remembered that we had always gotten burned by following the consensus. In the past we found it very difficult to get out of ten-year loans when we saw very aggressive pricing for our assets or if interest rates fell, so after looking very carefully at the situation, I came to the conclusion that short-term interest rates were going to stay low for a very long period of time. We would be well compensated for borrowing on a variable-rate basis while others were borrowing on a fixed-rate basis. This strategy would allow us to go in with a starting rate advantage of at least 1.5 percent per year, assuming interest rates didn't move for a while. And we would have much greater flexibility to do something different with our debt or property after the first year.

This strategy paid off. LIBOR stayed in a very, very low range (between roughly twenty and thirty basis points) for a few years (and still is the case as of this writing). Meanwhile, fixed-rate loans were higher than the rates we were paying.

The following is adapted from a 2011 analysis that applied many of MMT's principles to what was taking place at the time. The long quoted excerpts that follow are from the book *Since Yesterday: The 1930s in America* by Frederick Allen Lewis. I found such striking parallels between then and now with regard to the economic, political, and social climate that it helped me greatly in terms of helping me to anticipate the Obama administration and Congress's reaction functions. The economic carnage and societal outrage in the aftermath of the outrageous lending decisions and business practices of the financial sector necessitated very aggressive government intervention via spending, regulation, and the pursuit of those who committed grievous offenses.

A Political Calculation

The economic system had pulled out of its sinking spell of 1929–33 only to become a chronic invalid whose temperature was lower now in the mornings but showed no signs of returning quickly to normal. Americans were getting used to the fact that nine or ten million of their fellow-countrymen were out of work. . . . The economic headquarters of the country had not only moved from Wall Street to Washington, but apparently had settled down there for an indefinite stay. . . . No major decision could any longer be made in Wall Street without the question being asked, "What will Washington say to this?"

All this development of the Federal power the Republicans viewed with loud alarm; yet with such an air of inevitability did the growth take place that one wondered whether the Republicans, should they come to power, would be able to reverse the trend. It seemed likely that the difference between the two parties would be that one of them, in moving toward the concentration of power in Washington, would move with the throttle open; the other, with the brakes on . . . Surely, the visitor from Mars would have said, these parties which so denounce each other are virtually as Tweedledum and Tweedledee. . . . Bitterly the campaign progressed. Not since 1896, certainly, had public feeling run so high over an election. To hear angry Republicans and angry Democrats talking, one would have supposed the contest was between a tyrant determined to destroy private property, ambition, the Constitution, democracy, and civilization itself, and a dupe of Wall Street who would introduce a fascist dictatorship.

I was convinced in 2011 that all roads were leading to Washington, DC, as they did in the 1930s (and as Allen so eloquently described). With this being the case, it was important to have a sense of where things were headed, because most major industries, and especially housing, were going to be impacted by decisions coming out of the Capitol. From a CWS perspective, decisions regarding how the record postwar deficit was handled would have an indirect impact on the supply and demand for apartments and borrowing costs.

I will work backwards and tell you how I think the story would unfold from my 2011 vantage point and will then provide you with more details to support my assertions.

Here were the "givens" as of 2011:

1. The private sector was cutting its debt load, especially the financial sector.

2. Households needed to rebuild their savings.

3. Housing remained oversupplied as foreclosures continued to take place in large numbers.

4. Monetary policy was nearly impotent, with short-term interest rates at near 0 percent.

5. Inflation was very tame given global overcapacity, especially with regard to labor.

6. Tax rates were relatively moderate on a historical basis, so there was less impact from cutting them.

7. There were approximately 13.3 million people unemployed.

There was no choice but for the federal government to fill the hole created by the deleveraging (debt reduction) by issuing new Treasury securities (deficit spending) to prop up demand in the economy and to provide more savings (Treasury securities) to households.

I know this sounds heretical, but we had to come to terms with the fact that blood was being drained from the US economy by debt repayment and by a desire for more savings (which constitutes a leakage of spending out of the system). So the last thing we needed to do was apply leeches (tax increases) to the patient in order to drain more blood or reduce the flow of blood (cutting spending) when there was enormous savings and demand deficiency. The only way to shrink the deficit would be through growth, and we could not achieve growth through tax increases and spending cuts. Those could only occur down the road once

US households and consumers had rebuilt their balance sheets and had enough confidence to spend and invest. This would mean, in turn, that businesses could invest and hire, passing the baton from the public sector to the private sector. In the meantime, deficits would help keep demand more elevated in the US economy and provide additional savings (US Treasuries) to a savings-deficient household sector mired in overleveraged real estate, stagnant incomes, a weak job market, and tight credit. It would take many years to achieve the handoff to the private sector, and if we worried about the deficit we risked running into the same problem that FDR faced when he sought to balance the budget in 1937, which precipitated a terrible recession that gave up approximately 67 percent of the growth (in industrial production) that had been achieved in only nine months from the bottom of the Great Depression.

My concern about the effects of deleveraging on the American economy was echoed in early 2012 by one of the largest and most successful hedge fund firms, Bridgewater Associates. In a January 3, 2012, *Wall Street Journal* article about Bridgewater, the following points are conveyed which reinforce the deleveraging thesis:

> Robert Prince, co-chief investment officer at Bridgewater, and his managers at the world's biggest hedge fund firm are preparing for at least a decade of slow growth and high unemployment for the big, developed economies. Mr. Prince describes those economies—the US and Europe, in particular—as "zombies" and says they will remain that way until they work through their mountains of debt.

> "What you have is a picture of broken economic systems that are operating on life support," Mr. Prince says. "We're in a secular deleveraging that will probably take fifteen to twenty years to work through and we're just four years in."

In Europe, "the debt crisis is [a] long ways from over," he says. The economic and financial morass will mean interest rates in the US and Europe will essentially be locked at zero for years.[2]

Yet, despite what I thought was the solution (i.e., keeping the spigot open) I didn't believe the political will existed to do this at the levels we needed. Austerity and deficit reduction seemed to be the publicly stated intentions of both political parties. If this truly came to pass, then I believed it would result in a more slow-growing economy than would otherwise be the case, and would also lead to continued low interest rates for many years to come. For this reason, a fair number of our more recent financing decisions had been to select variable-rate loans. This may seem odd, given how attractive fixed-rate loans were and that short-term interest rates had nowhere to go but higher. As stated earlier, however, there are some distinct advantages with variable-rate financing:

- There are much lower-cost prepayment penalties, providing us with greater flexibility in the event we want to sell or refinance the property.

- With fixed-rate loans we would require buyers to assume the financing, which lessens the buyer pool because most purchasers prefer to structure their own financing rather than having it forced on them.

- These loans also have conversion features that allow us to switch to a new, fixed-rate, longer-term loan if we think it makes sense at the time.

- There is typically a 1 to 2 percent starting rate advantage versus the prevailing fixed-rate alternative at the time the loan is

2. Tom Lauricella, "Bridgewater Takes Grim View of 2012," *Wall Street Journal*, Jan. 3, 2012, http://online.wsj.com/articles/SB10001424052970204368104577136531481564726.

originated. We thought this advantage should remain in place for at least two years based on stated Federal Reserve policy of holding rates where they were through at least mid-2013. Indeed, this was the case, as we all now know.

What could move short-term rates higher? Albert Einstein said, "Everything should be made as simple as possible, but not simpler." In the spirit of Einstein, I think it simply comes down to jobs, and job growth is very difficult to generate when the private sector is deleveraging (cutting its debt burden). Based on my research, I realized that the economy had become much more "financialized." Whether we like it or not, we have been heavily dependent on Wall Street, and I think this is one of the reasons behind the 2011 Occupy Wall Street movement. When humans feel powerless and perceive themselves to be at the mercy of ignominious forces, they want to lash out and regain some sense of power, control, and dignity. There has also been a stunning and unprecedented drop in financial debt since 2008, as a result of the near-cataclysmic collapse in the global financial system that began with the subprime mortgage debacle that spread to housing, the stock market, high-yield debt, and finally Europe. Why is this important? Because the more "financialized" we have become, the more connected our job creation has been to the growth of debt in the financial sector.

When financial debt grows, the unemployment rate drops; and when it contracts, unemployment expands . . . until both exploded in opposite directions with the global financial meltdown that commenced in late 2007. Although the bleeding has stopped, if Prince of Bridgewater is correct, then we still have another ten years or so to go before the deleveraging ends.

What Has Filled the Void?

With such drastic debt reduction occurring in the private sector, something had to fill the void, lest we spin into a deflationary vortex of depression. This is where the federal government stepped in with unprecedented post–World War II spending. It is for this reason, as previously mentioned, that I began this chapter with excerpts from the extraordinary book *Since Yesterday: The 1930s in America*, as I believe there is no better parallel to today than what took place in the 1930s, which was preceded by the boom of the 1920s, akin to our 2000–2007 period. I attempt to look at the world as realistically as I can, I study history to find the best parallels, and I do my best to assess how things will unfold. My aim is to determine what we can best do to prosper from the circumstances (or to avoid the risks that may materialize). Earlier I stated that we needed to continue to keep the spending spigot on to avoid spiraling downward economically and, ultimately, socially.

It doesn't take a really keen observer to see that when unemployment goes down, so does federal government borrowing; and when unemployment goes up, so does federal government borrowing. This should convey to those worried about the deficit that the solution is simple: get people working again. More jobs mean more tax revenues, heightened economic activity, and less expenditure on unemployment insurance plus the other collateral costs of people being out of work (i.e., crime, health problems, psychological issues, and hunger).

In 2011 I asserted that we had a large deficit because of a jobs problem, and not the other way around. The only way to reduce the deficit was through economic growth and (this is where the analysis comes back to our borrowing strategy) low interest rates for a long period of time. Interest rates kept lower than the rate of economic growth would allow us to grow our economy much more rapidly than the rate of growth of our debt, while still allowing us to rack up huge deficits over the next five to ten years or so to cushion the blow of private sector deleveraging. By suppressing interest rates, the Federal Reserve could do its share to keep the cost of borrowing low for the federal government—so that it could carry out an orderly transition back to the private sector over the next decade, to once again become the engine of growth.

What about inflation? It was nothing to worry about given the tremendous excess capacity we had in the global economy, especially when it came to labor.

So what was I worried about and continue to be worried about today? Austerity! The following chart shows how much the Obama administration has cut public payrolls relative to other administrations. This has been something that has held the economy back more than would otherwise be the case if public payrolls had followed a similar trajectory as other presidents.

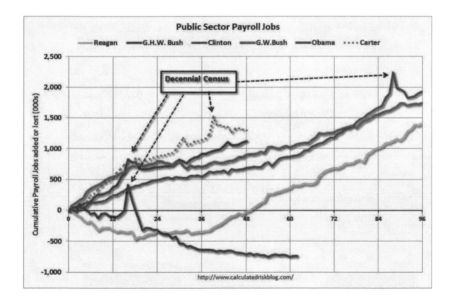

As apartment owners we would expect mild austerity to keep more people renting, to allow for interest rates to remain low, and to enable us to continue to increase rents provided there is not a meaningful increase in supply of new apartments. Overall, I am hard pressed to think of an industry as well positioned as ours to benefit from an environment of mild austerity.

I will sign off from this chapter with one more excerpt from *Since Yesterday*, to draw a parallel from the past that I think is still relevant today. It illustrates why large deficits will be with us for many years to come, whether we like it or not:

> Throughout these early years of the New Deal the levels of prices and wages and the structure of corporate and private debt were being artificially supported by government spending—or, to put it another way, by the failure of the government to levy high enough taxes to take care of the spending. If it had been possible for the law of supply and demand to work unhindered, prices and wages—and the volume of corporate and private debt—would theoretically have fallen to a "natural" level and activity could have been resumed again. But it was not possible for the law of supply and demand to work unhindered. In a complex twentieth-century economy, deflation was too painful to be endured. Hoover had set up the RFC because the banks couldn't take it; Roosevelt had set up the Federal relief system because human beings couldn't take it.

Chapter Thirteen

LET THE NUMBERS DO THE TALKING

An ounce of performance is worth pounds of promises.

—*Mae West*

It's taken some lengthy background to get to this point. There is nothing more to add except to quantify how we did. We had many hypotheses, but at the end of the day, investors only care about our performance. Was this truly a Munger Moment? I believe the numbers support this contention. Since 2010 we have had forty-eight properties in our portfolio that we still owned through 2013. Here is a table showing what we produced in 2013 versus 2010 and the percentage change in major categories:

	2010	2013	% Change
Revenue	$141,451,000	$170,392,000	20.5%
Expenses	(65,396,000)	(73,289,000)	12.1%
Net Operating Income	76,055,000	97,103,000	27.7%
Capital Expenditures	(8,874,000)	(17,433,000)	
Adjusted NOI	67,181,000	79,670,000	18.6%
Principal	(4,687,000)	(8,061,000)	
Interest	(51,060,000)	(41,950,000)	(17.8%)
Cash Flow	11,433,000	29,659,000	159.4%
Debt Balance	907,446,000	964,542,000	
Approx. Avg. Int. Rate	5.62%	4.35%	

The power of healthy NOI growth and a minimal change in debt service allowed us to increase cash flow dramatically during these three years, resulting in much healthier distributions to our investors, strong gains in equity value, and the ability for us to reinvest significant sums into our properties with more in store for the next few years.

In addition to the very impressive growth in our same store portfolio, we also accomplished the following between 2010 and 2014:

- We acquired forty properties exceeding $1.3 billion in total capitalization.

- We refinanced thirty-four properties.

- We sold fifteen properties.

- We recapitalized our eighteen-property GE Capital portfolio in which we bought GE out of eleven assets and sold seven in a transaction exceeding $700 million.

- We initiated our first pooled investment and have completed six of them, raising over $90 million.

- We increased distributions significantly as cash flow grew dramatically due to strong operating results and lower interest rates.

- Regarding development, we
  - built four properties and leased them up;
  - funded two development partnerships;
  - broke ground on four properties; and
  - transitioned one property into predevelopment.

We have dramatically shifted our debt to variable-rate loans since 2011. Since that time we put seventy new loans in place for acquisitions and refinances (exclusive of the GE recapitalization), and fifty-one of them were variable with an average rate of less than 2.6 percent. We now have approximately 57 percent variable debt, or $1.1 billion out of approximate total debt of $1.93 billion.

In 2009 and 2010 we at CWS began to recognize that we were on the precipice of a Munger Moment amidst such chaos, fear, and uncertainty permeating our society, economy, and investors in the wake of Lehman Brothers, AIG, and the subprime meltdown, among other challenges.

We were not going to let this once-in-a-lifetime opportunity slip through our fingers due to fear or being overburdened by having to solve problems. Our experience with other downturns gave us the wisdom and courage to make sure we had the right resources to clean up the past while also embarking on an amazing journey to recraft our future in tremendously positive ways. We had cultivated enough goodwill with investors to have them trust our judgment and ability to execute on taking advantage of the opportunities, such that we ended up with the fuel (capital) to monetize the madness that was unfolding. Mike Engels went into action and used his extraordinary leadership skills, intellect, and sense of urgency to make sure we had the right resources to ensure our focus on keeping our investors informed and on fielding a team to capitalize on the investment opportunities we saw unfolding. Steve and I took the lead in negotiating with our lenders and communicating with our investors about the challenges and opportunities and in raising money from them to take advantage of the Munger Moment. It was another example in CWS's history of how an effective partnership could work. The three of us were very open and honest with each other about what we thought needed to be accomplished, and then we aligned on a game plan and divided and conquered to do what was necessary to make it happen.

It is hard to overemphasize what a remarkable transformation took place at CWS. Mark Twain said, "It ain't what you don't know that gets you into trouble. It's what you know for sure that just ain't so." We looked at the environment and saw many people who were absolutely convinced that the world was coming to an end, the United States was turning into a socialist country with uncontrollable spending and bank bailouts, and the Federal Reserve was printing so much money that interest rates would go through the roof and the dollar would collapse. What they thought was so just wasn't true, from our perspective. It was these dogmatic beliefs of many investors that helped convince us that if we moved quickly and aggressively, then we could capture a tremendous amount of value without incurring much risk, especially since we had a long-term investing horizon. To summarize, this is what we believed that was quite different from the consensus in 2010:

- The economy would recover because of government involvement, not in spite of it.

- Cap rates would revert back to 5 to 6 percent on average when liquidity started to return, which we projected to be within a relatively short period of time.

- The Fed was not printing money. It was carrying out an asset swap that essentially exchanged interest-bearing, longer-dated Treasury securities for cash that paid very little interest.

- Interest rates would stay low for a very long period of time, allowing for tremendous opportunities in utilizing low-cost, variable-rate loans.

- Construction lending would come to a screeching halt due to the pressures on the banking system, leading to minimal supply concerns starting in 2011.

- Renter household formations would dwarf newly created owner-occupied households as the mortgage market would tighten up; student loan debt would be burdensome in qualifying for mortgages; individuals would need to build and rebuild their credit by going to where the jobs were while also, in many instances, taking advantage of vibrant urban living that was reemerging throughout the United States and was much more renter focused than ownership oriented.

- All of these combined to set up a supply-and-demand relationship in the apartment industry that would be incredibly favorable to apartment owners, particularly in faster-growing cities like those we were invested in (Dallas, Fort Worth, Houston, San Antonio, Raleigh, Charlotte, Atlanta, and Denver).

We believe that we have done a very good job of monetizing this opportunity, as the list of accomplishments and portfolio performance from earlier shows. We have grown the organization while still keeping our unique culture and fierce commitment to serving all of our customers in an effort to enhance their lives "The CWS Way." We have developed a very strong reputation in the apartment industry as a very high-quality management company, a great place to work, and a very thoughtful and successful investment management firm.

In the end, we followed Munger's formula quite closely. Our patience and clearheadedness in the past enabled us to avoid being bogged down with problems such that we were able to look up and out and see if there could be opportunities as a result of the carnage of the Great Recession. Our experience with other downturns, along with our unique analysis on the 1920s and 1930s and our study of the work of Richard Koo and Warren Mosler and other important sages, convinced us that the odds of success were dramatically in our favor. Now all we needed was the courage and resources to take advantage of it. And take advantage we did, as the financial results show. We were able to monetize the tectonic shift of discarding the misguided notion of an ownership society to a more balanced approach allowing for the reemergence of more of an urbanized, renter nation.

*   *   *

Although some of my guiding thoughts and principles have been sprinkled through the book, up until this point the focus has been on conveying some of the most impactful personal and business experiences and some biographical information to show how we were prepared to recognize and capitalize on the Munger Moment and other tectonic shifts. It would not feel complete, however, having written a book called *The Philosophical Investor,* without communicating my philosophy in more detail, which is the goal of the last part of the book. As in the earlier sections, I am not without some important guides in helping me generate and convey these thoughts and ideas. Some notable ones include Shakespeare, Richard Feynman, Robert Hunter, Van Morrison, and, of course, Schopenhauer.

Part III

LESSONS LEARNED

from this

LONG, STRANGE TRIP

Chapter Fourteen

THE PHILOSOPHICAL
INVESTOR'S PHILOSOPHY

To be yourself in a world that is constantly trying to make you
something else is the greatest accomplishment.
—*Ralph Waldo Emerson*

I must tell you right off the bat that this chapter is going to be unusually short. For some of you, that may be great news, while for others who are more obsessive-compulsive about consistency among the chapters with regard to length, I am deeply sorry. As I finished the manuscript I realized that there was the distinct possibility that the book could end up containing twenty chapters. For some reason that made me really happy. It just seemed so elegant to have twenty, as opposed to nineteen, chapters. The initial feedback was that this chapter was too short. My heart sank. I had three choices: (1) lengthen it (which I'm technically doing with this digression and confession); (2) embed it in an existing chapter, which would have shattered my dream of having a book with an even twenty chapters; or (3) keep it as is and stick to my obsessive guns. I chose a combination of numbers one and three. I just couldn't let it go. So with that background, the purpose of this chapterella (a short chapter, as a novella is a short novel) is to introduce you to the last section of the book.

I have done my best to convey what I believe was a unique and interesting journey and its culmination: recognizing and taking advantage of one of the greatest investment opportunities in a very long time, one that was right in our sweet spot. It wouldn't feel complete, however, unless I were able to go and take this body of experience from the micro- to the macro-view by conveying some of the philosophical insights and lessons that I have gathered on this long, strange trip. As Schopenhauer said,

> The first forty years of life furnish the text, while the remaining thirty supply the commentary; and . . . without the commentary we are unable to understand aright the true sense and coherence of the text, together with the moral it contains and all the subtle application of which it admits.

Schopenhauer goes on to say that when we're in the middle of it, the swirl of our daily lives, we rarely have time to reflect on where we have been, why we did what we did, and what unifying force might have been guiding our actions. While what Schopenhauer had to say about this was quite lengthy, I strongly recommend taking the time to read it carefully, because it is quite powerful.

> Again, just as the traveler, on reaching a height, gets a connected view over the road he has taken, with its many turns and windings; so it is only when we have completed a period in our life, or approach the end of it altogether, that we recognize the true connection between all our actions,—what it is we have achieved, what work we have done. It is only then that we see the precise chain of cause and effect, and the exact value of all our efforts. For as long as we are actually engaged in the work of life, we always act in accordance with the nature of our character, under the influence of motive, and within the limits of our capacity—in a word,

from beginning to end, under a law of necessity; at every moment we do just what appears to us right and proper. It is only afterwards, when we come to look back at the whole course of our life and its general result, that we see the why and wherefore of it all. When we are actually doing some great deed, or creating some immortal work, we are not conscious of it as such; we think only of satisfying present aims, of fulfilling the intentions we happen to have at the time, of doing the right thing at the moment. It is only when we come to view our life as a connected whole that our character and capacities show themselves in their true light; that we see how, in particular instances, some happy inspiration, as it were, led us to choose the only true path out of a thousand which might have brought us to ruin. It was our genius that guided us, a force felt in the affairs of the intellectual as in those of the world.

I have tried to use my skills, through discovery, effort, and teaching, to create wealth for those who have honored me with their trust and confidence. And by doing this I have been able (at times) to find deep satisfaction in helping to make a positive difference in many lives. These include our investors, employees, residents, friends, and family. Joseph Campbell said, "Money experienced as life energy is indeed a meditation, and letting it flow out instead of hoarding it is a mode of participation in the lives of others." I have made an effort to use my skills to create more positive energy in life-enhancing ways, one of which is via earning very competitive rates of return on capital invested with us.

I have a beautiful family, incredible business partners and coworkers, and interesting and highly accomplished friends. I work in a business that offers flexible housing alternatives for thousands of people, have been part of a firm that has provided a livelihood for hundreds of people, have traveled the world, and have been able to live in one of the most beautiful places on the planet. I am a very lucky person and extraordinarily grateful for all of the gifts in my life.

In the last part of the book, I feel that it is incumbent upon me to share some of the lessons learned from my journey. I intend to cover the following:

- knowing oneself (with the help of Shakespeare)
- healthy ecosystems and how these characteristics can help investors evaluate investment management firms like CWS
- benefits of real estate, especially apartments
- the power of partnership (take two) and an update on Jacob
- the benefits of variable-rate loans
- true wealth and avoiding the "No Wonder Years"

When all is said and done, I have hoped to leave the world a little better off than I found it by using my unique gifts to enhance the lives of those who have come to trust and rely on me in some form or fashion. I have been lucky to find a career, company, and partners that have been an ideal match for my gifts. As the brilliant writer and teacher Julia Cameron said, "What we really want to do is what we are really meant to do. When we do what we are meant to do, money comes to us, doors open for us, we feel useful, and the work we do feels like play to us."

Let's complete this journey with some of the most important ideas that have helped me transform wisdom into wealth. And you will come to learn that when I use the term "wealth," it goes far beyond the financial realm. My definition ties together the most powerful ideas conveyed in this book in a way that can open the possibility for living a life of great abundance.

Chapter Fifteen

KNOW THYSELF: NOT HARD, IF YOU FOLLOW THE BARD

Know thyself and to thine self be true.
—*William Shakespeare*

As I have come to learn, there truly is very little new under the sun. The timeless wisdom of the world's geniuses are as applicable today as when they were first conveyed, as Schopenhauer so brilliantly explained. With this in mind, what new could I bring to the table when it came to some of the most important lessons I have learned about myself, others, and human nature in general? Really there was nothing, especially when one has a body of work like William Shakespeare's to pull from. The Oracle of Delphi said "know thyself," which is one of the most important requirements for successful investing. As I have said previously, I view one of CWS's main jobs as protecting people from themselves. Shakespeare has been invaluable in this, because we have to make sure that we at CWS don't get tripped up by our blind spots, incentives, and constraints into making suboptimal decisions for the people who entrusted us with their hard-earned money. We need to make sure we protect them from themselves and not from us!

In 2012, I marked the twenty-fifth anniversary of my career at CWS. Having just returned from a great trip to England, where my final days in Stratford-upon-Avon (the birthplace of William Shakespeare) elevated my interest in the Bard, I realized that to create works still relevant and widely consulted nearly four hundred years after one's death is truly remarkable. I hope that—on a much smaller scale, of course—this book has some relevance for many years to come. As Shakespeare's Cleopatra said, "Give me my robe, put on my crown; I have / Immortal longings in me."

My daughter took the trip to Stratford with me and was reminded of it when she said that she was reading *Macbeth* in class at school. She picked up on one quotation in particular, and wanted to know if we (her parents) knew it. It was this one: "[Drink] provokes the desire, but it takes away the performance."

I must confess that I was a little taken aback and that I hadn't heard it before. But I was proud that she had such good retention of what she was learning. That quotation is as true today as it ever was, of course, which just goes to show that human nature doesn't change (or physiology for that matter). And in case you're wondering, the aforementioned quotation had no influence on me deciding to subtitle this chapter "Not Hard, If You Follow the Bard."

My twenty-fifth year at CWS seemed to be a good time to reflect on the past quarter century. I must say we had quite a journey over the twenty-five years, encompassing all aspects of comedy, tragedy, and history. Maybe those categories should have been the three parts to this book.

Continuing the Shakespearean theme, I note that Shakespeare's plays have five acts, so I'll replicate that structure in the organization of this chapter—with Shakespearean quotes peppered liberally throughout, where relevant.

On paper, our job as investors looks pretty simple: avoid investments that can result in the permanent loss of capital (as per Buffett's definition of risk), identify those that offer the appropriate return for the risk borne, evaluate them, get them capitalized, execute on the business plan, and deliver competitive cash flow and appreciation for the risk incurred—which ultimately includes making good sale decisions. Yet this is obviously easier said than done, since not many firms have been able to survive and prosper for more than forty-five years as CWS has. So, while far from perfect, we must be doing enough things right to have navigated the turbulent seas that have been described throughout the book. And just to make sure you didn't forget some of the notable storms, here are some of them again, in no particular order:

- the 1987 stock market crash
- the savings and loan crisis
- formation of the Resolution Trust Corporation (RTC)
- two Iraq wars
- Afghanistan
- 9/11
- the dot-com collapse
- the NASDAQ falling by 80 percent
- the housing boom and crash
- the bankruptcy of Lehman Brothers
- government conservatorship of Fannie Mae and Freddie Mac
- the European crisis
- the implosion of Long-Term Capital Management
- the Asian crisis of 1997–1998

So . . . how are we still standing?

There is a tide in the affairs of men,
Which, taken at the flood, leads on to fortune;
Omitted, all the voyage of their life
Is bound in shallows and in miseries.

Now, without further "ado," let's move on to those five acts that I promised you.

Act I: Know and Be Thyself

To be successful requires avoiding self-sabotage. We must recognize blind spots that can get in the way of evaluating situations honestly and realistically, and we must notice character defects that can trip up even the best-intentioned people.

SCENE 1: AVOID SELF-DELUSION, LEARN YOUR BLIND SPOTS

> *With mine own weakness being best acquainted.*

If we ignore that which can cloud our judgment, then we have lowered our chances of success. It is important to know what our blind-spot triggers are. It is also vital to surround ourselves with people who see the world differently than us, and who are not afraid to tell us what they believe is the truth, even if it's something we don't want to hear.

> *Marry, sir, they praise me, and make an ass of me. Now my foes tell me plainly I am an ass; so that by my foes, sir, I profit in the knowledge of myself, and by my friends I am abus'd; so that, conclusions to be as kisses, if your four negatives make your two affirmatives, why then the worse for my friend and the better for my foes.*

SCENE 2: KNOW YOUR CHARACTER DEFECTS

We all have weaknesses and compulsions that, if not held in check, can inhibit our growth and success and, at their most extreme, can even destroy us. No one is immune, so it is important to know what our susceptibilities are and to do all we can to shield ourselves (and others) from them.

> *We are all men,*
> *In our own natures frail, and capable*
> *Of our flesh; few are angels.*

SCENE 3: CULTIVATE INDEPENDENT THOUGHT AND TAME OUR EMOTIONS

Unfortunately, human beings are subjected to waves of fear and greed that often lead them to buy at the top and sell at the bottom. It is imperative to develop independent thinking . . .

> *Let every eye negotiate for itself,*
> *And trust no agent.*

. . . and to tame one's emotions so that we don't get caught up in the madness of the crowd.

> *I will not jump with common spirits,*
> *And rank me with the barbarous multitude.*

It is critical that we try to keep as much perspective as possible when times are good, to not get too giddy, and to focus on what could go wrong.

> *You should have feared false times when you did feast.*

SCENE 4: HONESTY AND INTEGRITY

It goes without saying that these are vital for long-term success.

This above all: to thine own self be true,
And it must follow as the night the day
Thou canst not then be false to any man.

Act II: Prepare Thyself

Adversities in life are inevitable, so it is vitally important that we be as prepared as possible to deal with them in as healthy a manner as possible. In addition, there are some people who experience great fortune yet are as ill-prepared to handle it as those who run away during times of challenge.

This ambitious foul infirmity,
In having much, torments us with defect
Of that we have; so then we do neglect
The thing we have.

SCENE 1: HEALTH

Good health is critical to making sure we don't drop our guard and make poor decisions when dealing with challenging times. This incorporates physical, emotional, mental, and spiritual health.

Our bodies are gardens, to the which our wills are gardeners.

A major contributor to one's health is a good conscience, which allows one to be more present, calm, and serene.

A peace above all earthly dignities,
A still and quiet conscience.

SCENE 2: GRATITUDE

Gratitude is a key component of happiness. It helps keep us in the now, it cultivates joy and appreciation for those people and things in our lives, and it can be a source of strength when times get tough.

> *What we have we prize not to the worth*
> *Whiles we enjoy it, but being lacked and lost,*
> *Why then we reck the value, then we find*
> *The virtue that possession would not show us*
> *Whiles it was ours.*

SCENE 3: POWER OF MIND

It is essential to cultivate a disciplined and powerful mind that does not allow negativity to take hold. We must realize the power we have to reframe our circumstances in a more positive, growth-oriented way.

> *Every bondman in his own hand bears*
> *The power to cancel his captivity.*

> *For there is nothing either good or*
> *bad, but thinking makes it so.*

SCENE 4: VISUALIZE SUCCESS

Seeing is believing, and being able to visualize a future, desired state is an important tool in our arsenal for managing through adversity and unexpected fortune.

> *We are such stuff*
> *As dreams are made on.*

SCENE 5: FAMILY

A great support system goes a long way toward navigating the ups and downs of business and investment cycles. I am fortunate to have an amazing wife and two wonderful children who help keep me grounded and intentional.

Wife and child
Those precious motives, those strong knots of love.

Act III: The Power of Adversity

No investor can avoid adversity. It is impossible for everything to go as planned.

Oft expectation fails, and most oft there
Where most it promises.

It is critical that we have the strength, courage, tenacity, and perseverance to battle through the tough times, to learn from them, and to come out on the other side wiser and stronger.

Let me embrace thee, sour Adversity,
For wise men say it is the wisest course.

SCENE 1: NEED FOR A POWERFUL PURPOSE

In order to find that reservoir of strength to tap into when times get tough, it is vital to be living through the prism of a powerful guiding purpose. This helps us look beyond ourselves and enables us to realize that what we are enduring will be worth the sacrifice and will make us stronger.

There's a divinity that shapes our ends,
Rough-hew them how we will.

SCENE 2: DEAL WITH BAD NEWS EARLY

I have learned that when we are off plan, it is important to communicate the bad news early in a manner that is comprehensive, understandable, and transparent.

Honest plain words best pierce the ear of grief.

Investors detest negative surprises and, while they may not like the news we deliver, they appreciate our being open with them and treating them as partners. We have always attempted to communicate with our investors in the same manner we would wish from another company managing our money, especially when things turn out differently than expected.

I must go and meet with danger there,
Or it will seek me in another place,
And find me worse provided.
Defer no time, delays have dangerous ends.

SCENE 3: STAYING POWER AND PERSEVERANCE

You can't survive the downturn and capitalize on the recovery if you do not have financial and emotional staying power. It is vitally important to have sufficient financial reserves to support investments that need additional capital so as to not have to sell under pressure or lose properties to lenders. Unfortunately (or fortunately) we have had a lot of experience in this regard, and, each time, we have not only been able to generate a competitive return on the new money invested, but we have also been able to protect the original capital.

> *Thrift, thrift, Horatio. The funeral baked meats*
> *Did coldly furnish forth the marriage tables.*
> *Our purses shall be proud, our garments poor.*

SCENE 4: DON'T BE TOO HARD ON YOURSELF

I have learned over the years that life hardly ever unfolds quite the way we expect it to. If our intentions are good, then we cannot wallow in too much self-flagellation over what we should have done differently.

> *We are not the first*
> *Who with best meaning have incurred the worst.*
> *Things without all remedy*
> *Should be without regard: what's done is done.*

At CWS, we are definitely our harshest critics, because we hold ourselves to very high standards, we hate to lose, and we particularly don't want to let down our investors.

> *The private wound is deepest.*

We view the money our investors have entrusted with us as "stored labor," and we honor what went into earning the capital that has been invested with us.

> *Uneasy lies the head that wears a crown.*
> *I live with bread like you, feel want,*
> *Taste grief, need friends—subjected thus,*
> *How can you say to me, I am a king?*

Act IV: Recognition, Courage, and Action

It is vital to get the big trends right, because that allows us to have a framework to view developments as they unfold. I have learned to pay particularly close attention to investment bubbles: how they form, how to spot them, and the consequences when they burst. By doing so, we better position ourselves to avoid losing money and to take advantage of the opportunities that arise in the aftermath of a financial dislocation.

Show me one scar charactered on thy skin: Men's flesh
preserved so whole do seldom win.
Nothing will come of nothing.

SCENE 1: UNDERSTAND CYCLES

Knowledge of cycles is invaluable for determining when we should be fearful (i.e., when others are greedy) and when we should be greedy (i.e., when others are fearful). It is critical for me to have some guiding paradigms through which I can view the world and envisage how things will unfold economically, to help separate the signal from the noise. It has been said, "History doesn't repeat, it rhymes." No two cycles are ever exactly the same, because the excesses don't always materialize in the same parts of the economy. For example, with the overinvestment in homeownership having caused the most recent financial crisis, there was no way homeownership would be the source of recovery as it had in so many previous cycles. I am working from three very powerful models that influence how I see economic events unfold.

- Richard Koo's *Balance Sheet Recession*;
- Modern Monetary Theory; and
- the sectoral balances approach from the Levy Institute that breaks down where spending and savings are coming from in the economy.

These have led me to believe that renting will be vital for many years to come, interest rates will stay low for a very long time, and there is nothing to be fearful of in terms of our large federal deficits. In fact, the bigger risk is government tightening through spending cuts and tax increases.

How many ages hence
Shall this our lofty scene be acted over,
In states unborn, and accents yet unknown?

SCENE 2: EVALUATE RISK AND REWARD

It is important to keep a cool head and evaluate opportunities objectively, as free from bias as possible. The first objective is to not lose money, and once this is a reasonable probability we can then turn to making money. It's important to avoid errors of optimism (believing the good times will continue indefinitely) as well as errors of pessimism (because tough times are usually when the best opportunities are to be had).

When clouds appear wise men put on their cloaks.
When great leaves fall, the winter is at hand;
When the sun sets, who doth not look for night?
Untimely storms make men expect a dearth.
Hercules himself must yield to odds;
And many strokes, though with a little axe,
Hews down and fells the hardest-timbered oak.

SCENE 3: COURAGE AND ACTION

If to do were as easy as to know what were good to do, chapels had
been churches, and poor men's cottages princes' palaces.

It takes courage to make an investment, especially when there is a great deal of pessimism and negative sentiment. Yet these are often the best times to take action because prices are cheap due to a lack of capital and investor/lender disinterest. Those who correctly assess the opportunity and who access the capital only need then the courage to take action.

Be bloody, bold, and resolute.
Be swift like lightning in the execution.

The opportunity to strike is often fleeting, because eventually investors realize that things are not as bad as they thought, the future looks brighter, and prices are compelling. This leads to more competition and higher prices, so it is important to act when the stars are aligned.

Courage mounteth with occasion
You come most carefully upon your hour.
Make use of time, let not advantage slip.

At the end of the day, it feels good to take action. It is easy to delay, overanalyze, and be consumed by fear. What separates those who make money in the long run from those who don't is the ability to seize the opportunity when the timing is right—without concern for what others think.

Action is eloquence.

SCENE 4: EXECUTION, SIMPLICITY, AND FOCUS

It is important to have strong capabilities to execute on compelling opportunities. The more focused an organization is on its core competencies, the better its chances of success.

Take but degree away, untune that string,
And hark what discord follows.

Put thyself into the trick of singularity.
Never anything can be amiss
When simpleness and duty tender it.

Act V: Love the Learning and Playing the Game

As mentioned previously, I love puzzles: finding the pieces that go together and seeing the picture unfold over time. Life isn't as well organized as a puzzle or game, however. We have to discover what those pieces are and how they fit together in a chain of cause and effect. I have found that approaching the world of investing like this makes it much more interesting, and it improves the probability of success, because I want to know why something worked or why it didn't. I then use this information to form hypotheses.

Learning is but an adjunct to ourself
And where we are learning likewise is:
Then when ourselves we see in ladies' eyes,
Do we not likewise see our learning there?
What many men desire! that "many" may be meant
By the fool multitude, that choose by show,
Not learning more than the fond eye doth teach,
Which pries not to the interior, but, like the martlet,
Builds in the weather on the outward wall,
Even in the force and road of casualty.

SCENE 1: CHESS METAPHOR

The Nobel Prize–winning physicist Richard Feynman described learning physics as figuring out the rules of chess by observing how pieces move and interact rather than being given the rules, pieces, and board at the outset. This is one of the most influential descriptions for me in terms of the mindset and sense of wonder and discovery we need if we want to master anything in life. We need to learn how things work (cause and effect) so that we can develop an intuition. We also need a broad domain of knowledge to see how the game will unfold before others do. By developing this sixth sense we can avoid the pitfalls that ensnare others and thereby take advantage of opportunities that others don't see as clearly or don't feel confident pursuing.

> *This fellow is wise enough to play the fool,*
> *And to do that well craves a kind of wit.*
> *He must observe their mood on whom he jests,*
> *The quality of persons, and the time;*
> *And like the haggard, check at every feather*
> *That comes before his eye. This is a practice*
> *As full of labor as a wise man's art;*
> *For folly that he wisely shows is fit,*
> *But wise men, folly-fall'n, quite taint their wit.*
> *Blest are those*
> *Whose blood and judgment are so well commeddled*
> *That they are not a pipe for Fortune's finger*
> *To sound what stop she please.*

SCENE 2: PATIENCE—ONE STEP AT A TIME

Long-term success requires patience. Opportunities tend to come in waves created by a buildup of financial excesses that lead to easy money pushing up asset prices. This leads, in turn, to more easy money creatively structured to finance higher and more aggressive valuations. Eventually the unstable foundation gives way, leading to a collapse and the destruction in its wake. To take advantage of the opportunities that materialize out of the carnage requires having capital, an opportunistic mindset, the ability to execute in taking advantage of the opportunities, and the courage to take action in the face of the widespread pessimism that a burst bubble leaves among market participants. To have these capabilities, however, necessitates having avoided the problem to begin with, so that you can be on offense when everyone else is on defense. This requires discipline, perspective, a conservative orientation, a deep understanding of cycles, knowledge and recognition of how bubbles form and burst, and an organization that can slow down while others are going fast and still keep on firm financial footing and able to retain its talent.

> *To climb steep hills*
> *Requires slow pace at first.*

It is surprising how much success can accrue if you're willing to develop a plan and establish principles you adhere to in terms of the risk you're willing to take, the opportunities you are comfortable investing in, and the savings goals you are trying to achieve.

> *What you cannot as you would achieve,*
> *You must perforce accomplish as you may.*

There is no need to try to get rich quick or take enormous risks to earn large, quick returns, because it usually backfires. Remember, a 50 percent drop in the value of one's investment requires it to go up by 100 percent just to get back to even.

> *Wisely and slow; they stumble that run fast.*

SCENE 3: ENJOY THE JOURNEY

If you are constantly focused on the destination, then it is difficult to build up sustainable levels of satisfaction and joy from the hard work of the journey. Mastery requires digging more deeply and deriving great satisfaction out of incremental improvement, learning what the right things to do are and doing them right, and recognizing that you're traveling down the right path. Later, you can look back and see how far you've come while still having many miles of beautiful terrain ahead.

Things won are done; joy's soul lies in the doing
To business that we love we rise betime
And go to't with delight.

*   *   *

I look forward to someone reading this in 2412 (or perhaps 2052 would be satisfying as well) and finding value in it.

Chapter Sixteen

HEALTHY ECOSYSTEMS

*Luck is a very thin wire between survival and disaster, and not
many people can keep their balance on it.*
—*Hunter S. Thompson*

Nature is fascinating to me. What I find so interesting is how systematic and interconnected it is and how species and ecosystems evolve. I naturally (pun intended) wanted to see if there were any lessons that could be applied to investment firms like CWS (and ourselves individually) from the characteristics of healthy ecosystems. After doing some research, I came across the following simple characteristics that made a lot of sense to me. A healthy ecosystem

- is active;
- maintains its organization and autonomy over time;
- has substantial vigor to quickly recover or utilize stress in a positive manner; and
- reaches full life expectancy.

Active

*The young man knows the
rules but the old man knows the exceptions.*
—*Oliver Wendell Holmes*

As I reflected on these qualities, I found that these are also great principles by which to help manage CWS. It is a cliché, but firms need a sense of vitality and creative energy to be ever present, or stagnation and dull thinking can take over. Bob Dylan said that "he not busy being born is busy dying," and in many ways I think this is true for investment management firms. This doesn't mean they should be always focused on acquiring more assets when market conditions are not right. In fact, one form of growth is looking at the world from a very rational point of view and determining what the right course of action is. When the risks outweigh the rewards, then it is time to hit the brakes; and when rewards far exceed the risks, then go like a bat out of hell.

I also believe it is important that the key members of the firm are keen on personal growth. Mastery requires deep domain knowledge and an ever-growing understanding of small nuances that can help one spot anomalies and develop a keen intuition for risks and opportunities that others may not be cognizant of. In addition, because most people cannot be nourished only from work, it is important for the firm to encourage personal growth by supporting education and hiring people with interests beyond their jobs that can help recharge their batteries. In short, we believe that meaningful results and organizational improvement can only occur through people who are

- highly motivated;
- focused;
- grounded by a strong set of values; and
- working in a healthy team environment with people-centered leadership driven by a magnetic pull in a compelling direction.

It is important to have a balance between fresh blood and more seasoned leadership principally for the reasons cited in the quotation above. I think Schopenhauer explained it pretty well when he wrote the following in his usual somewhat blunt, curmudgeonly, negative tone:

> If the chief feature of the earlier half of life is a never-satisfied longing after happiness, the later half is characterized by the dread of misfortune. For, as we advance in years, it becomes in a greater or less degree clear that all happiness is chimerical in its nature, and that pain alone is real. Accordingly, in later years, we, or, at least, the more prudent amongst us, are more intent upon eliminating what is painful from our lives and making our position secure, than on the pursuit of positive pleasure. I may observe, by the way, that in old age, we are better able to prevent misfortunes from coming, and in youth better able to bear them when they come.

Maintains Its Organization and Autonomy over Time

One of the great fortunes of CWS has been our ability to remain independent for over forty-five years, despite experiencing a tremendous amount of growth. It is very typical for real estate firms to access outside capital for individual projects or to fund portfolio growth. Often, however, the principals of the firm are required to coinvest with their partners in these projects and funds. Many principals come to the point where the growth exceeds their ability to meet the coinvestment requirements, and they either have to slow down or bring in partners who buy into the firm in exchange for this growth capital. Our experience has been that many principals often regret selling a portion of their firm. They miss the ability to act much more independently, diverging interests can arise, and cultural differences can reveal themselves and lead to more time spent dealing with clashes than building the business. Our autonomy has allowed us to maintain and build a very strong culture infused with a consistent set of values and operating principles. It has also allowed us to build a very strong and cohesive team comprised of many long-term employees (average corporate tenure is over nine years) matched with very talented younger people who bring tremendous energy and fresh ideas to keep us old fogies on our toes and challenged.

The long-term orientation that has resulted from remaining autonomous has allowed us to attract and retain great people as we make every effort to invest in the systems, training, and support staff to allow them to excel at their jobs. On the surface, buying, building, and managing apartments and reporting to investors seems easy, yet it is far more complicated as one gets a deeper understanding of the business. It is now very technology-centric and requires a number of powerful systems that need to be integrated and coordinated. We have been able to maintain an organization "The CWS Way" that we believe has given us great advantages to react quickly when problems arise and to see opportunities materializing earlier than otherwise would be the case.

Substantial Vigor to Quickly Recover or Utilize Stress in a Positive Manner

It's quite remarkable to think how well the United States bounced back from Pearl Harbor and September 11, just to cite two examples of national catastrophes. Investment firms will almost always face very challenging times at some point in their life cycle. Virtually every great investor has experienced terrible downturns. This has happened to the likes of George Soros, Julian Robertson, Michael Steinhardt, Stanley Druckenmiller, John Paulson, and even Warren Buffett; all of them went through a period of underperformance. Here are some of the questions that must be addressed:

- How do you handle it when your investments are not performing well?

- How do you manage your investor communications?

- Were the errors due to systematic weakness or failure, poor judgment, or bad luck?

- What do you do to try to learn from the situation?

Most great investors come back very strongly after stumbling, and they take a hard look at what mistakes they made in order to minimize the chances they arise again in the future.

We have had our share of challenges at CWS, as has been chronicled throughout the book. To reiterate, we purchased properties in technology-oriented cities between 1999 and 2001, when the dot-com bubble burst and massive job losses ensued. To compound the problem, we financed many of our properties with long-term, fixed-rate debt at high interest rates that could not be refinanced for many years due to cost-prohibitive prepayment penalties. We dealt with the problems head-on, informed our investors of the challenges we were facing, quantified the amount of additional capital we estimated the properties would need until the high-cost loans could be refinanced or the properties sold, came up with plans to monitor our performance, and communicated regularly with our investors so they knew what was happening.

As one of our founders Bill Williams likes to say, "Out of the hottest fire the strongest steel is formed." And this was very true for us at CWS. Our willingness to deal with the problems in a professional, straightforward manner and our successful resolution of each situation—in ways that not only returned the additional capital plus a competitive rate of return but also preserved the original capital plus a profit—earned us tremendous goodwill from our investors. They concluded that we were the type of organization they would want to be in the foxhole with if times got tough again, and we feel the very same about them. We are convinced we are stronger and wiser for the challenges we have faced. It is inevitable that we will experience more difficulties, but our job is to maintain the wherewithal and margin of safety to make sure we can recover quickly from it and ultimately be stronger as a result.

Reaches Full Life Expectancy

There is not much to say here other than that this tends to contradict some of the old rock and roll notions, memorialized by The Who and Neil Young, of "Hope I die before I get old" and "It's better to burn out than to fade away." Apparently CWS is quite an anomaly for having been in business for more than forty-five years. According to the Bureau of Labor Statistics, 65 percent of small businesses make it to two years while only 44 percent make it to five years. Yet in our economy, all of this creative destruction serves to create a pretty vibrant and dynamic ecosystem that has lasted over 230 years while producing incredible amounts of wealth and dramatically improved living standards. Of course our system is not perfect, and far too many people are barely making it. Still, it does remain the envy of the world and generally seems to have all of the characteristics of a healthy ecosystem.

At CWS we have been very fortunate to have survived and prospered as we head toward our fifth decade of being in business. We have tried to focus our attention in areas where we can analyze and take advantage of opportunities that others may miss or dismiss. We constantly question ourselves to make sure we are assessing threats and opportunities with a clear head. We insist that our people be supported in the ways necessary for them to excel at their jobs and provide excellent service to our customers. We make sure our investors are being served in ways that help them meet their financial goals and give them confidence about investing with CWS, and they receive information that is timely, relevant, and accurate.

As you think about your life, do you find that you have the characteristics of a healthy ecosystem?

- Do you feel in control of your own destiny?
- Are you operating from a clear purpose?
- Do you feel proactive—or reactive?
- Do you exercise?
- Do you have healthy ways of releasing stress and tension?
- Do you have a set of values to help guide your actions?
- How do you handle stress?
- Do you see challenges as potential opportunities, or can they subsume you?

These are just a few basic questions to stimulate some provocative thought. Presumably if the answers are generally favorable, then you'll have dramatically increased the odds of living to full life expectancy (adjusted, of course, for the genes we've inherited and for the environment in which we have lived).

Since I'm wrapping up with the topic of living a full life, I'll end with a quotation from Virginia Woolf on the longevity of words:

> Since the only test of truth is length of life, and since words survive the chops and changes of time longer than any other substance, therefore they are the truest. Buildings fall; even the earth perishes. What was yesterday a cornfield is to-day a bungalow. But words, if properly used, seem able to live forever.

Perhaps this book will last far beyond my life, the life of our buildings, and perhaps even CWS.

Chapter Seventeen

THE BENEFITS OF REAL ESTATE

The avoidance of taxes is the only intellectual
pursuit that still carries any reward.
—*John Maynard Keynes*

Real estate is the one investment category that every individual must use in some form or fashion in his or her lifetime. Whether as a place to live, an office to work in, a store to shop in, or a place to store some of our larger possessions, real estate will always be in demand. This has historically made real estate a very good way to store, preserve, and grow wealth. This is the case for well-located properties that are maintained well, because real estate is typically a byproduct of economic and demographic factors. The United States, particularly in dynamic cities with a well-educated workforce, is able to innovate and grow over the long term, despite periodic setbacks. Real estate naturally benefits from this growth.

You Value Illiquidity

As I mentioned in the introduction, I like to say that CWS helps save people from themselves. Many of our investors recognize that successful investing is tough to do over a long period of time. By having money managed by CWS or firms like ours, investors hopefully lessen the risk of getting in their own way, either because they're bored and don't have enough to do, they are not interested in monitoring their investments, they're indecisive, they lack discipline, or they tend to be impulsive with their investment decisions. Not that we're perfect by any means, but if we do our job right, then hopefully investors can achieve better outcomes than they otherwise would, with a lot less worry. Illiquid investments also have a better potential to allow one's capital to compound by having it invested longer in strong real estate investments with durable cash flows that the sponsor (CWS or others) controls.

Tax Benefits

Often most, if not all, of the cash distributions can be sheltered from current taxes due to deductions for depreciation.

In a 1031 exchange, property owners that meet certain IRS requirements can continuously defer paying taxes associated with gains generated by selling properties if they reinvest their proceeds via 1031 exchanges. This can allow for tremendous pre-tax wealth creation.

Real estate can be an excellent estate-planning tool. Distributions made over the years, along with depreciation deductions, build up an increasing potential tax liability when it comes to time to sell. This makes using the 1031 exchange a very powerful and attractive wealth-preservation vehicle. At some point, after the investor passes away, his or her heirs can inherit the investment(s) based on the fair market value of the investment, less any discount for owning an illiquid, minority interest. This can wipe out most, if not all, of the ever-growing tax liability that had been building up over the years while the investor was alive. The heirs now own the investment typically at a much higher tax basis that will result in a lower gain on sale when the investment liquidates. In addition, to the extent the estate of the deceased was large enough to have to pay estate taxes, this burden can be lessened by applying the illiquidity/ minority discount when it comes to valuing it for estate tax purposes.

Leveragable Asset Class

Most commercial real estate loans are nonrecourse, meaning there is no liability to the borrowers for repaying the loans, provided no illegal acts were carried out that would result in a loss to the lender. The lender can only look to the collateral of the property or other pledges made by the general partner or affiliate.

Using borrowed money can magnify the returns, because loans only have a fixed claim on the cash flow and sale proceeds and do not participate in the profits. Thus, if the investment earns a greater return than the cost of the debt, then the investor's return will be magnified.

It also allows the investor to purchase a larger property than he otherwise could. This makes it much more efficient to manage and provides for a higher return potential, because more of an increase in revenues should be able to fall to the bottom line as compared to a smaller property.

The purchase of a larger property using borrowed money allows for more depreciable assets per dollar investment, thereby providing more shelter of one's distributions from immediate taxation.

Some lenders allow borrowers to borrow more money if the property's performance has improved. This is particularly helpful when a property could benefit from a significant investment to upgrade it. Without debt, the burden would fall on the current investors to fund the capital needed to carry this out. The right lender and loan structure, however, can allow for the advance of this additional capital.

Yield-Oriented Investment

Real estate is typically purchased to generate current dividends that are typically higher than what is available in the stock or bond markets. This is the case because most properties are limited in terms of expanding their capacity to generate more revenue in any way other than by raising rents. It is rare that more units can be created. Given this, real estate investors tend to want approximately half of their total return to come from dividends and the rest from capital appreciation.

Tangible Asset

Owning property is obviously tangible and is unique because of the owner's ability to improve upon it and add value.

Potential Inflation Hedge

Real estate has generally proven to be a hedge against inflation. As excess money is created, it needs to find a home, and real estate is one of the most desired asset classes when this is the case. Apartments are particularly well suited, because the average lease term is approximately eleven months, so it's easy to reprice the apartments in an environment of escalating rents given the relatively short lease terms, especially when compared to office, retail, and industrial properties.

Lacks the Volatility of Daily Pricing

We value our investments once a year as compared to freely tradeable securities whose prices fluctuate minute by minute. Not worrying about daily valuations can take a lot of the emotion out of investing and allow one to focus on adding value each day without being distracted by highly volatile market fluctuations.

Direct Control of Cash Flows

I believe that having directly owned and managed properties over the years has made the men and women of CWS much better decision makers and businesspeople. We have to deal with real-world problems, rather than evaluating management teams from afar as many stock and bond portfolio management teams do. We are more grounded and can use our vast amount of experience to evaluate opportunities and risks and separate the signal from the noise. We can also take direct action to add value to our investments, because we control the cash flows.

Why Apartments?

We've talked a lot about the advent of the renter nation at CWS for a number of years. When the housing bubble was in full force, we were pretty sure that there would be a day of reckoning, as loans were originated on a huge scale to individuals who had very little margin of safety if their income were interrupted and/or home values declined. Sure enough, the house of cards collapsed, and the housing market went down in flames.

The following graph shows new single-family sales going back to 1959 and existing home sales (resales) going back to 1999. We can see how frothy the housing market became for both new homes and resales from 2003–2007. New home sales subsequently collapsed and remain at depressed levels. Meanwhile, the mortgage market remains tight, the price of many resale homes is low enough to discourage the building of new ones, the labor market is soft, and consumer psychology is weak.

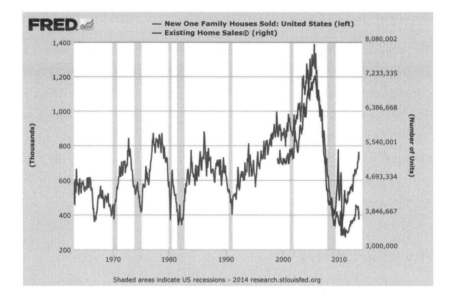

This has led to a dramatic reduction in the homeownership rate, although one could argue that it has only gotten back to more historical levels and should never have gotten as high as it did.

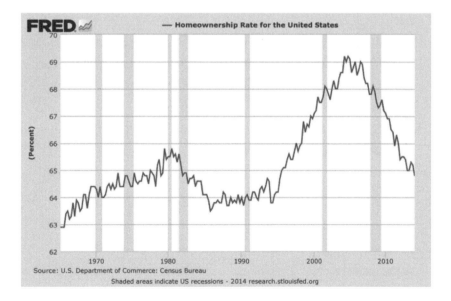

The principal reason homeownership has dropped is due to young people losing their homes or not buying homes as they did—as the following graph shows.

Homeownership Rates by Age of Family Head

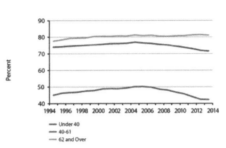

Source: *http://www.stlouisfed.org/publications/itb/articles/?id=2481*

Sam Zell is known for making bold statements, not all of which turn out to materialize. Yet, he did say something that I think has a lot of merit. In a recent *Bloomberg* article covering the Milken Institute Conference that took place on April 29, 2014, he said that the homeownership rate could drop to 55 percent due to younger people delaying marriage and choosing to rent for longer periods of time. Zell is quoted as saying:

> "The deferral of marriage has such a staggering impact on real estate and I just don't think people focus on it," said Zell, 72, whose Chicago-based Equity Residential is the largest U.S. apartment landlord. "I don't think the multifamily market has ever had a better set of future demographics."[1]

1. John Gittelsohn, "Zell Says Homeownership Rate to Fall as Marriages Delayed," Bloomberg News, April 29, 2014, http://www.bloomberg.com/news/2014-04-28/zell-says-homeownership -rate-to-fall-as-marriages-delayed.html.

The following charts help show how this trend has been evolving over a long period of time.

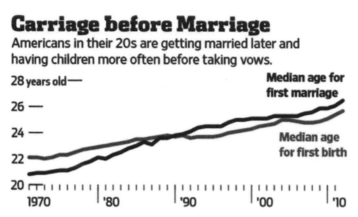

Sources: U.S. Census Bureau, Centers for Disease Control and Prevention and the National Center for Family & Marriage Research. The Wall Street Journal

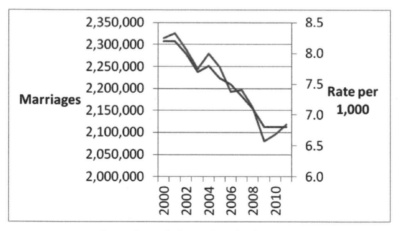

Source: Centers for Disease Control and Prevention

One fascinating trend that has also been developing for a while is the degree gap between females and males. There are many more female college graduates than males, and some speculate that this will continue to lead to fewer marriages or more delays in the future, as women with college degrees may be less inclined to marry men without them. If this letter from a Princeton mom is any indication, then this could be a powerful trend.

> I am the mother of two sons who are both Princetonians. My older son had the good judgment and great fortune to marry a classmate of his, but he could have married anyone. My younger son is a junior and the universe of women he can marry is limitless. Men regularly marry women who are younger, less intelligent, less educated. It's amazing how forgiving men can be about a woman's lack of erudition, if she is exceptionally pretty. Smart women can't (shouldn't) marry men who aren't at least their intellectual equal. As Princeton women, we have almost priced ourselves out of the market. Simply put, there is a very limited population of men who are as smart or smarter than we are. And I say again—you will never again be surrounded by this concentration of men who are worthy of you.
>
> Of course, once you graduate, you will meet men who are your intellectual equal — just not that many of them. And, you could choose to marry a man who has other things to recommend him besides a soaring intellect. But ultimately, it will frustrate you to be with a man who just isn't as smart as you.
>
> Here is another truth that you know, but nobody is talking about. As freshman women, you have four classes of men to choose from. Every year, you lose the men in the senior class, and you become older than the class of incoming freshman men. So, by the time you are a senior, you basically have only the men in your own class to choose from, and frankly, they now have four classes of women to choose from. Maybe

you should have been a little nicer to these guys when you were freshmen?

If I had daughters, this is what I would tell them.[2]

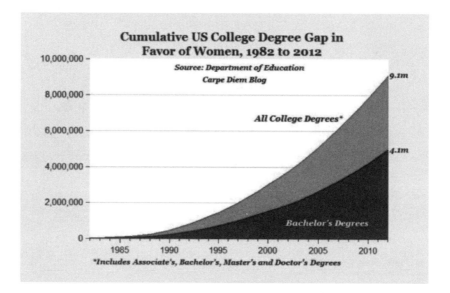

Approximately 41 percent of children are born to single mothers, and the odds of getting married lessen as educational level drops. Only 12 percent of those women with college educations have first births out of wedlock, while the rate is 83 percent for high school dropouts. This looks to pose a looming challenge, as there are currently 9.1 million more degreed women than men and 3.1 million more in college now, as the chart above shows.

I believe that Zell is right that the apartment industry has a very bright future beyond demographics, which I'll touch on shortly. Before doing so, I thought I would share a couple of graphs that depict how

2. Guest Contributor, "Letter to the Editor: Advice For the Young Women of Princeton: The Daughters I Never Had, The Princetonian, March 29, 2013, http://dailyprincetonian.com/opinion/2013/03/letter-to-the-editor-advice-for-the-young-women-of-princeton-the-daughters-i-never-had/.

amazingly strong the rental market has been since 2007 or so. The first chart shows the amount of rental income flowing to individuals. It's clear that the amount of rental income has exploded since 2007. Clearly it has been good to be a landlord.

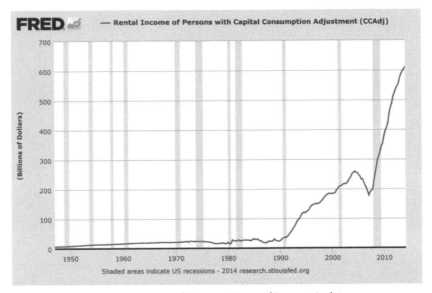

Source: U.S. Department of Commerce: Bureau of Economic Analysis

The second graph shows an index of inflation-adjusted expenditures for rental housing over a long period of time. It's clear that it shows a consistent uptrend, but this is not surprising, because the United States population has grown steadily for a long time, so the demand should be increasing. From an investment standpoint, apartments and rental housing have generally been a good investment in terms of providing some inflation protection with growth over a long period of time.

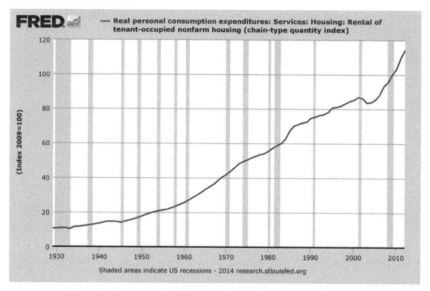

Source: U.S. Department of Commerce: Bureau of Economic Analysis

Beyond delayed marriages, the rental market should be supported by the large amount of student loans that individuals have taken out, particularly those in their prime renting years, aged eighteen to twenty-nine. Approximately 40 percent of student loans are to people younger than thirty. In addition, many older people have taken out loans as well, having gone back to school during the recession. Most of these loans are now backed by the federal government, as the following chart shows.

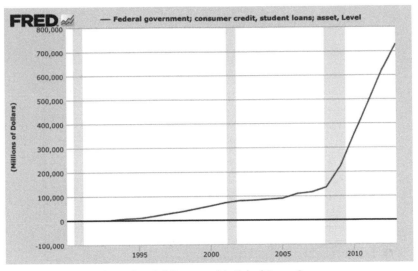

Source: Board of Governors of the Federal Reserve System
2014 research.stlouisfed.org

The performance of these loans is deteriorating as well, which doesn't bode well for future credit ratings for many of these delinquent borrowers. In addition, the delinquency is probably closer to double the reported rate, since about half of the loans are in the deferment phase in which interest payments can be paid down the road, presumably when there is more earning power. As evidence of this, according to the Federal Reserve Bank of New York, the delinquency rate for those under thirty was 8.9 percent as of the end of 2012 (the latest data) but 16.1 percent for those between forty and forty-nine, presumably with very little deferral of payments allowed in this age cohort.

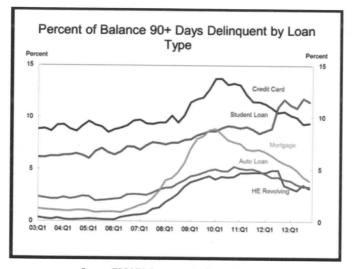

Source: FRBNY Consumer Credit Panel/Equifax

Unfortunately, incomes have not been rising meaningfully, as more of the economic output is accruing to capital in the form of profits and dividends. The following chart shows the growing gap between incomes and productivity (proxy for output):

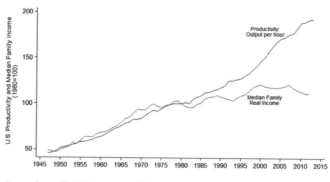

Source: houseofdebtblog.org @profsufi & AtifRMian, Data source: BLS, CPS

As the average required credit scores have risen since the downturn, the trend does not look very favorable for first-time homebuyers to enter the market in any meaningful fashion. They're generally lacking the credit, down payments, and incomes. This should keep people renting longer than they otherwise would, especially combined with the other factors cited previously.

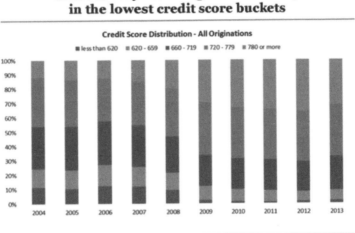

Source: www.lpsvc.com February 2014 Mortgage Monitor

Apartments have proven themselves to be an asset class that has staying power. While individual properties can face obsolescence and deteriorating location fundamentals, renting will always be in demand. And from what I can tell, the demand fundamentals should remain quite strong for a number of years to come.

Chapter Eighteen

THE POWER OF PARTNERSHIP, TAKE TWO

*Marriage is not a love affair, it's an ordeal. It is a religious
exercise, a sacrament, the grace of participating in another
life. . . . Successful marriage is leading innovative lives together,
being open, non-programmed. It's a free fall: how you handle
each new thing as it comes along. As a drop of oil on the sea, you
must float, using intellect and compassion to ride the waves.*
—Joseph Campbell

When my son Jacob got sick, it had a profound impact on my wife, Roneet, and me. It was a true test of our partnership at home. And it was amazing to see firsthand how Roneet has a true gift to sustain herself with positive energy even in the darkest of times. In particular, she spent every waking hour focused on Jacob and his recovery and making sure he was situated to perform optimally in school and enjoy his experience. We also wanted to help him get into college, get a degree, and learn to be independent, productive, and happy. It has been a remarkable outcome, and Jacob is incredibly fortunate to have a devoted mother like her. It's a story that truly shows in extraordinary ways the power of love, intention, and commitment.

But what we soon learned, even as Jacob was heading to college, was that his younger sister, our daughter, Ariella, needed our attention as well. Our partnership was tested once again, this time not by a black swan health event, but by the need to bring an open mind to making choices regarding Ariella's education, growth, and life experiences. In the end, we were fortunate to have the resources to think outside the box and take unconventional actions along those lines.

But I'm getting ahead of myself. Let me rewind to the point where Ariella, who is three-and-a-half years younger than Jacob, was entering high school, just as Jacob was leaving for college. We had spent the prior decade focused intently on Jacob and his therapy, as he had to relearn how to walk and talk in addition to undergoing surgeries to help him heal. All the while, both Roneet and I continued to work—she was a buyer for the department store Nordstrom. It was a very busy life.

In the end, Jacob weathered the storm—which allowed us to see more clearly how special Ariella was. Even when she was in middle school, she tended to isolate herself a lot, spending hours and hours reading and writing in her room. We also began to get reports from school that she remained isolated there as well. Her vocabulary was off the charts, but school and her relationships there didn't seem to fulfill her in any meaningful way.

By the time she was in the fifth grade, it was clear we needed to do something different. Eventually, we learned from our dear family friend Darrell about the Pegasus school for gifted kids, so we enrolled her in this private school in Huntington Beach, which was about a thirty-minute drive from our house. This meant that each ride to school was an hour round trip, which was a hefty commitment in those days. It took some effort—they didn't normally allow new students to enter the sixth grade—but we got lucky and they accepted her. It turned out to be a great experience for Ariella, and she began to thrive in a more academically challenging environment. It also opened our eyes to new opportunities when it came to where she wanted to attend high school.

In particular, she was thinking about going to boarding school in general, and a girls' school in particular.

Now at this point in our lives, we were fortunate to have the resources to be able to consider paying a fairly hefty sum when it came to tuition for private school. So Roneet led the charge to find one that would suit Ariella. But the more Roneet researched the schools closer to home, the more convinced she became that those schools simply weren't good enough to warrant making that kind of investment. I also took her on a tour of private schools on the East Coast. While there were several good candidates there, it was hard for us to envision sending our daughter across the country by herself.

Then one evening, Ariella got in trouble with her mother—which was an especially rare event. Roneet took away Ariella's computer as punishment. And as we lay in bed, Roneet started poking around and reading the material that was on Ariella's computer. What she found was several documents that, at first, looked like books Ariella had downloaded. They were deep fantasy stories that were clever, interesting, and well written. But as she read them and saw how the author had put in cute notes to her readers like "I hope you're still reading this," Roneet realized that these were books that Ariella had *written*. Roneet started shaking, because it began to dawn on us that our daughter had a very special gift.

While Ariella wasn't happy to have her secret discovered the way it was, she quickly got over it and confessed to us how she had been posting her stories online at a site called Fictionpress.com and that she had quite a devoted following. Again, she was in sixth grade. That served as a wake-up call to us that we needed to find her an environment where she could feed her gift further—something that wasn't going to happen at just any regular school.

So we began to expand our search into Los Angeles, an area that both Roneet and I knew fairly well, since we both had attended UCLA. At an open house for a well regarded school, Roneet struck up a conversation with another mom who was very helpful in shedding light on what options were available. Once Roneet told this woman about Ariella and her writing, she said Ariella needed to go to Marlborough, referring to another prestigious school in the area.

Roneet and I visited Marlborough and loved it. I was particularly enamored by the fact that the school actually had a building, Munger Hall, to which Charlie Munger and his wife, who was an alumnus of the school, were the largest donors. Even better, Ariella was accepted.

The question then became, How do we make this work? If you know anything about Southern California, you know that the region is plagued by traffic—which meant that any kind of commute was simply implausible.

The answer, it turned out, was renting an apartment (renting is always the solution!) near the school as a way for Ariella to attend school and then return home to Orange County on weekends, with her mother shepherding her the whole way. Roneet's focus would be to stay with Ariella in Los Angeles, while I would come up a few times a week as my schedule permitted. We would also have to be in close coordination to make sure I could be in Los Angeles when Roneet needed to return to Orange County. Fortunately, technology and understanding partners have made this quite feasible from a CWS perspective during the days I have needed to be in Los Angeles. As you could imagine, it was difficult for all of us. But Ariella began to thrive. Her writing flourished and she was getting an amazing education, which made it a worthy investment all the way around.

Yet, we still had three years to go before she graduated. That got Roneet thinking—especially when the lease came up for the apartment we were in. While it was a nice place, though in a somewhat sketchy area, Roneet began to pitch me on the idea that if we were going to spend a lot of money, then why shouldn't we just buy a place of our own? This was in 2012, when the real estate market remained stuck in neutral: nobody was buying anything. But that meant that prices were relatively low, in a historical sense. Even so, I was skeptical as there wasn't much in that price range that would be both close to the school and nice enough for us to live in.

But Roneet, to her credit, pushed on and really educated herself on the opportunities in the market. She developed a keen eye for what was available and soon enough came upon a beautiful new condominium building south of Beverly Hills. It was perfect—it had a contemporary design, low HOA fees, and even a doorman—and it was too expensive for us. But Roneet kept tabs on it, and lo and behold, she saw that one of the units had dropped its price by 15 percent overnight—which brought it right into our range. This was the place, Roneet insisted. While I remained skeptical—would it be worth the investment in three years when Ariella graduated?—we eventually closed on the condo for significantly less than the sellers paid just a year earlier.

Well, that happened to be one of those personal Munger Moments for us. Just six months later, a similar unit to ours sold for 15 percent more than ours—and prices have gone up from there. We estimate that the value of the condo has gone up by almost the exact same amount that we will end up paying in Ariella's tuition—and that's even if we decide to sell it, because it might make an excellent rental, given its proximity to Rodeo Drive, Fox Studios, and Century City. The bigger point, though, is that we had the wisdom to know what we needed to do and the courage to take action on it—which has made our lives better as a result.

Intentions Matter

Roneet and I have learned that whenever we have put our kids at the forefront of our partnership, it somehow translates into our best decisions and outcomes. We didn't seek out an opportunity to buy a house in LA because it would make us money; we did it to give Ariella the best possible education we could offer. But I think when you put the emphasis on doing good deeds for your family and children, your intentions are more powerful and you can think more clearly, which results in greater rewards.

It's interesting to look back and see how clear those lessons became to us when it came to buying our current family home. We bought our third house in 1994 after trading up from our first two. It was Roneet's instincts (yet again) that led us there, and she made an offer on the house without me even seeing it, since I was in Washington, DC, on a business trip. But I have long admired Roneet's intuition when it comes to making big bets like that, based, in large part, on her extraordinary track record at Nordstrom and just because she seems to be right an awful lot! That third house we bought came close to doubling in value—which then allowed us to think about getting something even better.

Fast-forward to the fall of 2001. We had friends who lived on a beautiful street where Roneet would take the kids to swim. It was a private, gated street with nine homes on it. And it was also expensive. But one day our friend mentioned that one of the homes was for sale, and that if we were willing to make a noncontingent offer on it (meaning we would be willing to buy the house without making it contingent on us selling our other house first) then we could probably buy it. The problem was that we didn't have enough cash to buy one house without selling the other one. But that's when Roneet's intuition kicked in and she said to me, "We need to buy this house." So I went to Steve, my partner at CWS, and explained the situation and the opportunity. He loved the numbers of the deal and agreed to lend us the money (something we had to camouflage a bit by telling the seller that it was actually a loan from my mom). That was an extraordinary gesture on Steve's part (we paid him back in full shortly thereafter) and something for which we will always be grateful.

With the new house under contract, we put our existing home on the market, because we had no desire to carry two homes at once. We held our first open house on September 8 and several interested couples returned on September 10. We were both anxious about selling the house, so we weren't sleeping well—which meant that we were up early on the morning of September 11. You know what happened next. We happened to see it live on television, because we were up very early, West Coast time.

As you might remember, the terrorist attack that day made it feel like the whole fabric of the world was coming apart. I even wrote a letter—maybe the best letter of my life!—to the seller of the house we had just contracted to buy, asking for a reduction in the price because everything seemed so uncertain (there was no reduction forthcoming). Meanwhile, we were sitting on two houses and deeply worried that we might never sell our other home. Fortunately for us, we did sell it—though it took two months of sweating it out.

In the end, it was a fantastic deal for us. Not only did we land our family's dream home, we got it at a great price. We could sell our house today for probably double what we paid for it—which illustrates the power of a personal partnership to take advantage of these Munger Moments in our lives. On our own, neither Roneet nor I might have been able to tackle those opportunities. But by bringing our brains together, we have been able to navigate the challenges to achieve a successful result. That's not to say that every outcome will be a positive one. But I've truly come to believe that great things often result when you can truly tap the power of partnership.

This is a poem I wrote for Roneet on her fiftieth birthday:

We met on the stairs and you said you liked the color of my shirt
and I was thinking wow, what a beautiful looking dessert.

Events unfolded, one thing led to another
and somehow, someway we ended up with each other.
She went back to the OC while I finished at UCLA
yet I couldn't stop thinking of her every day.
An older woman with a younger man

boy was I lucky; I was putty in her hands.

While she took Nordstrom by storm in less than a year
I stumbled on my job at CWS with a lot of fear.
But without her incredible support
I would not have had such a successful career.

We got engaged on that 4th of July day
never fathoming the dragons we would have to slay.
A honeymoon from hell in which we were robbed the very first day
only to come home and find our condo ransacked away.

Family members getting sick and my dad passing away.
Still, nothing rocked our lives like Jacob on that fateful May day.
Our lives would never be the same yet Roneet gave everything she had
to make sure Jacob felt loved and should never feel sad.
He's been an incredible trooper and inspiration to us all
especially when he's on the court playing B-Ball.

Ariella comes around and there's no parenting book for someone like her
so funny, beautiful, enigmatic, and a reader that's for sure.
Traditional schools couldn't do it for her day to day
so when Jacob went to college we headed to LA.
It hasn't always been easy, I must honestly say,
but it's been quite an adventure each and every day.
Roneet is an incredible wife, mom, sister, and daughter
I guess that's why there's nothing I haven't bought her.

I love you and thank you for always being there
This has been an amazing journey and one I will always treasure
You are my best friend and I will love you forever.

Chapter Nineteen

GO VARIABLE, YOUNG MAN

You can't take the same actions as
everyone else and expect to outperform.
—Howard Marks

It has been my experience that most people are very uncomfortable purchasing real estate financed by loans with variable interest rates. They much prefer fixed-rate loans. They can sleep better at night, knowing they have taken interest-rate risk off the table. I have also found that there is no free lunch, as economists like to point out. While we at CWS like to differentiate ourselves in other ways when it comes to how we invest in the apartment industry, our emphasis on variable-rate loans is definitely the road less traveled. Although approximately 54 percent of our approximately $1.9 billion in debt is variable, of the last forty-nine loans we have put in place between 2011 and 2013, thirty-seven have been variable (as of this writing). We have ventured much more aggressively in this arena over the past couple of years.

This bias was well earned. Fixed-rate loans usually have very costly prepayment penalties if rates don't rise much and the yield curve remains somewhat steep. This makes refinancing these loans very cost prohibitive when interest rates drop, and properties become much more difficult to sell as they require buyers to assume the loans. This is suboptimal, as it forces one's capital structure on the purchasers, which serves to shrink the buying pool.

Roneet and I own four pieces of property, and all four are financed with variable-rate loans in which the interest rates can change monthly. Thus, I am definitely eating my own cooking, as we like to say. Why am I such a big fan of variable-rate loans versus fixed?

- Demographics
- Natural tendency to have long-term rates higher than short-term rates
- Structure of the monetary system
- Weak inflation pressures
- Investors are usually wrong
- Shadow rate suggests rates should be negative

Demographics

I have always thought that there was a relatively strong long-term correlation between labor force growth and interest rates. The faster the growth in the labor force and consequently employment, absent significant productivity gains, the more pressure on inflation—in theory—as the demand for goods and services should rise as a result of more purchasing power. This chart shows the close connection between the rolling ten-year growth rates of the civilian labor force and nominal GDP. The peaks occurred roughly between 1980 and 1982, which is when interest rates also hit some of their highest levels in US history. Since then they have been coming down for over thirty years. From a short-term interest rate perspective, they really can't drop any more, as rates are at 0 percent.

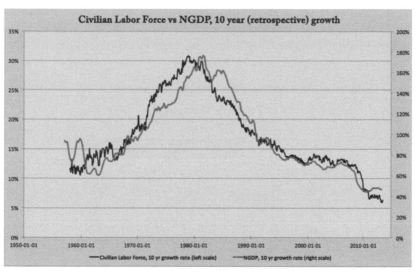

Source: http://www.interfluidity.com/v2/4561.html

The labor force has not been growing, and it is not expected to grow much for a while as baby boomers start to leave the workforce and are not replaced by as large of a population cohort.

Natural Tendency for Long-Term Rates to Be Higher than Short-Term Rates

I love data (goes back to my dice baseball days). I wanted to crunch the numbers and see how beneficial (or harmful) being variable would have been from when LIBOR (the index against which all of our variable loans are based) was created in 1986. Assuming there was no differential in spreads applied to LIBOR and Treasuries to come up with loan rates (this is not entirely accurate, but they're close enough to have this analysis be informative), then it should be easy to calculate whether LIBOR-based loans ended up being cheaper or more expensive than those based on seven- and ten-year Treasuries. I went back to 1986 and compared daily Treasury yields for seven- and ten-year maturities with how LIBOR performed over the next seven and ten years by averaging the daily yields. The results appear in the table below, and they're quite striking.

Thirty-Day LIBOR versus Seven-Year and Ten-Year Treasury Yields (1/86–10/24/14)

	Higher	Lower	Total
7 Year—Days	101	5,362	5,463
% of Time	1.8%	98.2%	100.0%
Average	0.21%	(2.07%)	(2.02%)
Worst Outcome	0.54%	0.00%	N/A
10 Year—Days	0	4,712	4,712
% of Time	0.0%	100.0%	100.0%
Average	N/A	(2.41%)	(2.41%)
Worst Outcome	N/A	(0.44%)	N/A

Approximately 98 percent of the time, variable-rate loans based on LIBOR would have outperformed those fixed based on seven-year Treasuries by having a lower cost of funds, and this goes up to 100 percent of the time over ten-year horizons. The worst outcome would have been paying approximately 0.54 percent more per year than the prevailing fixed-rate loan. Yet, the risk/reward was far more in favor of being variable, as the average positive result was cheaper by 2.07 percent per year, while the worst outcome was 0.54 percent more expensive. The results are even stronger for ten-year horizons, where the worst outcome was 0.44 percent better than fixed, while the average was 2.41 percent per year more favorable. Investors (and bettors) would kill for odds like these. Yet people remain skeptical because they think that rates have to go higher, and they remember the horror stories of the 1970s and early 1980s. So what about those times? How did being variable compare to fixed back then? Since LIBOR didn't start until 1986 and the ten-year

Treasury securities didn't start trading until 1953, I had to construct a slightly different dataset. I used three-month Treasury bills as a proxy for short-term rates and used the monthly averages versus the daily yields, since that is what was available for some of the Treasury yields.

Ninety-Day Treasury Bill Yields versus
Seven-Year and Ten-Year Treasury Yields (1953–1985)

	Higher	Lower	Total
7 Year—Months	88	110	198
% of Time	44.4%	55.6%	100.0%
Average	1.23%	(3.22%)	(1.24%)
Worst Outcome	3.18%	(0.01%)	N/A
10 Year— Months	230	163	393
% of Time	58.5%	41.5%	100.0%
Average	0.88%	(2.50%)	(0.52%)
Worst Outcome	2.14%	0.00%	N/A

Even during the inflationary, higher interest rate era of 1953– 1985, on average it was better to be variable than fixed. Granted, there was tremendous volatility and periods in which variable significantly underperformed fixed. Yet the times when variable was better were a lot more beneficial than those when fixed outperformed variable. The average outperformance was significantly greater than the average underperformance.

Finally, the poster child for low rates has been Japan. Despite having ten-year government yields of less than 1 percent, going variable has outperformed fixed 100 percent of the time since 1989.

Why are short-term rates almost always lower than long-term rates? For this we have to return again to MMT and the structure of the monetary system.

Structure of the Monetary System

The natural overnight interest rate is very close to 0 percent. Yes, you read that correctly. After Nixon closed the gold window in August 1971, the United States dollar became a fiat currency. It was backed by nothing and eventually was freely floating, with no obligation to peg the value of the currency to any other currency or commodity. In addition, the government did not borrow in foreign currencies. The currency has perpetual value, because taxes must be paid in that currency. As a result, the government has to spend that currency into existence in order to collect it via taxes. This gives it value, as the citizens will try to accumulate that currency to pay taxes.

Government spending creates reserves for the banking system. This has the effect of providing the reserves necessary to fund any deficits that may arise. It's really not even a funding mechanism, but a reserve management tool and a way for the government to generate interest income for savers. The important thing is that there will almost always be excess reserves in the system because of federal deficits and bank lending, since loans create deposits. Banks don't need to wait to have the necessary reserves to lend. They are constrained by having quality borrowers relative to their outlook for the future and capital requirements set by the Federal Reserve. When banks make a loan, they will credit the borrower's account, and miraculously, funds appear out of thin air. Now reserves are created, even if the borrower spends the money, since those dollars will flow to another depository institution.

Absent Fed intervention to support a policy rate or the central bank paying interest on reserves, banks will compete to lend out excess reserves. This will push overnight rates close to 0 percent. As previously mentioned, bond issuance and taxes drain reserves from the system. They don't need to fund the government. They are interest rate and demand management tools. This is very counterintuitive, but I do believe that MMT has accurately described how our monetary system operates. This knowledge has provided further support for my bias toward variable-rate loans due to the "natural rate" being closer to 0 percent, absent Fed intervention. Of course, the Fed could always raise rates, but rates do not need to be higher for any "natural" reasons other than to fight inflation. Yet from the chart below, based on the Cleveland Fed's inflation model, there do not appear to be any meaningful inflation pressures for the next thirty years.

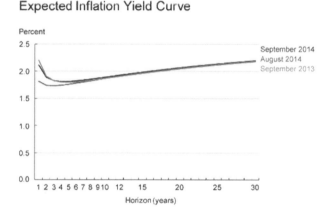

Source: Haubrich, Pennacchi, Ritchken (2012)

One of the counterintuitive results of lower interest rates is that there's a strong argument that by lowering the interest income in the economy it can reduce demand and buying power, which can serve to lower inflation over time. This is known as the Fisher Effect. The following chart shows the estimated decay of inflation to where the model anticipates inflation being, based on the Fisher Effect. It's quite a dramatic drop, and if it is anywhere near being accurate, then one would not expect interest rates on the short end of the curve to rise anytime soon.

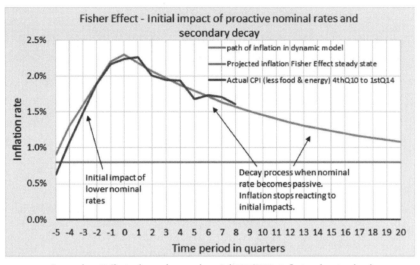

Source: http://effectivedemand.typepad.com/ed/2014/05/is-inflation-decaying.html

The following is a fairly esoteric graph that attempts to estimate what short-term interest rates would be if they could go negative. This is called the shadow rate. The chart shows how well this methodology tracked the actual effective federal funds rate. Based on the current estimate, the rate should be –2.89 percent (April 2014), the lowest rate in the fifty-plus years the model has been back tested.

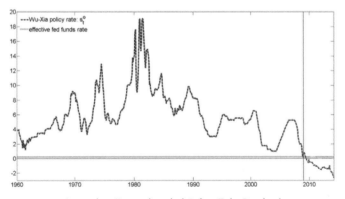

Source: http://econweb.ucsd.edu/~faxia/PolicyRate.html

Finally, this graph shows how wrong investors have been in predicting future short-term rates. The vertically oriented lines were investor predictions for rates and the bottom, and the relatively horizontal line is what has actually happened.

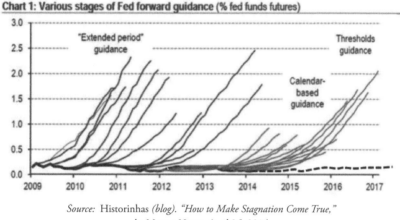

Chart 1: Various stages of Fed forward guidance (% fed funds futures)

Source: Historinhas *(blog). "How to Make Stagnation Come True,"
by Marcus Nunes, April 26, 2014.*

It has been my experience that CWS's emphasis on variable-rate financing (as well as for my personal real estate) has allowed us to access debt capital at a much lower average cost than most of our competitors. In addition, it has enabled us to maintain tremendous flexibility to sell or refinance properties at what we believe are opportune times without having to incur costly prepayment penalties.

It is very difficult for most people to be at ease not having their debt fixed. It is too uncertain and nerve-racking, especially if one fears the reemergence of inflation. I believe that very low inflation and slower growth is a much more probable outcome than higher inflation and faster growth, for the reasons articulated in this chapter. The calculations I have carried out (back to my dice baseball days, but this time with much more on the line) have shown how powerfully skewed the rewards are relative to the risk for variable-rate borrowers over the past twenty-eight years. I believe this will continue to be the case, and we will continue to swim upstream and finance most of our properties with variable-rate loans to the extent possible.

Chapter Twenty

WEALTH AND WONDER

The beginner sees many possibilities,
the expert few. Be a beginner every day.
—Zen proverb

Like most people who have come to love the game of investing, my intention has been to generate great wealth for those who have entrusted their money with CWS and me. A funny thing happened on the way to becoming the next billionaire investment sage: my definition of wealth expanded immensely beyond the financial realm. And while I am very proud of what I have helped accomplish over the years for our loyal cadre of investors with my partners and team at CWS, I have also come to learn so much more about myself, human nature, and what true wealth is by having gone through some powerful experiences in the realm of investing and in my personal life.

Now let me share with you what I think makes someone wealthy. Here goes.

> An individual possesses wealth if he or she has the wisdom to avoid catastrophic errors, the hunger to look within to correct and grow from mistakes, the resources (financial, physical, and emotional) to recover from setbacks, and the courage to seize opportunity, and through it all is able to experience life with love, compassion, joy, and wonder.

If I were to simplify it I would say: Wisdom, Reality, Resilience, Courage, and Authenticity. Think of the radio station WRRCA to help you remember it. I love rock and roll, so the acronym sounds like "W Rocka," which works for me! We have to have the capacity to get up after we have been knocked down or dazed, to see our contribution to little mistakes, to ensure we avoid the catastrophic errors (akin to a permanent loss of capital, in the financial realm), to build up the muscle of courage to avoid intellectual, emotional, and financial atrophy, and to live from our unique quiet centers so we can be present to fully experience the joys and sorrows of life.

I know that's a pretty heavy definition, but I do think it covers much of what makes for a very deep and meaningful life. It takes into account connecting with others, physical and emotional well-being, self-knowledge devoid of delusion, fortitude, and a spiritual component (wonder). While the definition does involve a financial aspect, meaning and joy rarely arise if money is the star around which our lives orbit. Ideally, it's a byproduct of a life that is well lived and balanced. Of course some people are wealthier than others; it's the rare individual who possesses all of these attributes. Most of us, however, do have some of them. The important thing about this expanded definition of wealth is the aspirational nature of it. It's designed to capture the possibility of what it means to live a really great life. Shift Happens; there's nothing we can do about that. What we can do, however, is do our best to make sure we don't cause negative shifts to happen to us because of self-defeating behaviors. We can approach the tectonic shifts and setbacks that do happen with strength and equanimity, we can seize those rare, life-altering opportunities, and we can do whatever is possible to experience it all with a sense of joy, wonder, compassion, and love.

If I were to convey a visual metaphor of my description of wealth, it would be of a salmon swimming upstream, going against the current. Coming the other way are all the other fish swimming with the current, expending purposeless effort, telling the salmon all the things it should be doing, criticizing it for going against the tide, and not understanding why it is working so hard. They represent the "thou shalts" of society, the expectations and groupthink that can pull us away from our quiet centers if we pay too much attention to this noise instead of our intuitive signals. The salmon is driven by a higher purpose, a powerful calling that allows it to pay little heed to the fish swimming in the other direction, as they offer it very little value. They're only distractions. The journey is often arduous, but the salmon knows it has no other path or calling. It's what the salmon was born to do. It has to be alert to predators, and if there are close calls, it must put those experiences in its memory bank and learn from any mistake it may have made to help avoid them in the future. Finally, the salmon must seize opportunities whenever possible to get to its destination more quickly or take advantage of moments to conserve energy when the conditions are just right. And throughout the journey, this salmon looks up and out with eyes of wonder; no matter what obstacles and setbacks it encounters, it accepts them as powerful building blocks and lessons to help it strengthen its muscles of resilience and courage, contributing to the journey's meaning and purpose. It also helps the salmon to connect with those mythic figures from the past that it can identify with and who give it strength; it can realize that what it is setting out to do has been done before, and the world is better off for these heroes having embarked upon and completed their journeys. It is now this salmon's time and place to do what they did for those today who are now counting on it.

Of course we're not salmon, but the most evolved species on the planet, with free will and extraordinarily powerful nervous systems. So what choices can we make and what habits can we form to feel more comfortable swimming upstream, developing the strength and resilience to embark on the journey and stay with it when times get tough? I mentioned earlier in the book that I thought most humans are reaction machines versus reflective, responsive individuals, and that this wiring can lead to suboptimal decision making, particularly in the investment arena. Given this, I also believe the following are immensely important to help improve our chances of gaining more wealth in our lives:

- We must do whatever is necessary to rewire our minds and behaviors toward a more reflective, responsive approach. This helps defuse reactive impulses from stimuli that can trigger self-sabotaging behaviors. We can then avoid catastrophic errors that ruin relationships, impair our physical and emotional health, devastate our finances and those of others, and can potentially cause loss of our freedom.

- We need a personality that requires very little external validation, yet possesses a strong inner drive. This allows us to produce outstanding results by tapping into our innate, deep curiosity to figure out how the pieces of the puzzle fit together. We can recognize that investing and life are games in which the rules and how to win are not given to the participants ahead of time; these can only be discovered over time through keen observation and independent thought.

- We must follow our bliss and engage in life in a way that allows us to find the capacity to operate from our quiet centers. Thus, we can more easily separate the signal from the noise, keep our eye on the prize, drown out the cacophony of all of the "thou shalts," and experience great joy and wonder from life while also offering those we serve our love and compassion.

I want to end the book with an emphasis on putting more wonder back in our lives. I must state right at the outset that this should be read in the spirit of "Do as I say, not as I do." I am a very analytical person who relies much more on my head than my heart, so this should be taken into consideration when reading this. I do feel much of the time, however, that I could benefit from Van Morrison's realization in his song "I Forgot That Love Existed" that life could be so much more fulfilling and meaningful if one's heart could do the thinking and one's head could learn how to feel.

*   *   *

As I have progressed through life and my career, especially in this digital age in which information is accessible instantaneously and at all times, it has become more challenging to be fully engaged in the present. Our brains are nourished by focus and concentration, so depriving them of this can be akin to starving them. The return on focus has never been higher, in my opinion. Concentration is a muscle that needs to be exercised. It has become so much more difficult to do this, and the risk of atrophy grows exponentially.

Many of us remember the show *The Wonder Years*. It was a touching show about a family that was by no means perfect and yet, somehow, someway, was always able to find a way to come together in the end, during what was seemingly a much simpler and joyful time. The show is told through the recollections of one of the characters in hindsight who is now an adult. He was able to look back very fondly on those times with great joy and wonder. Yet, there was always a hint of nostalgia and sadness that those were times that would never be reclaimed, and perhaps he never quite appreciated them the way he should have. I think Schopenhauer described this perfectly when he said:

> We are always living in expectation of better things, while, at the same time, we often repent and long for things that belong to the past. We accept the present as something that is only temporary, and regard it only as a means to

accomplish our aim. So that most people will find if they look back when their life is at an end, that they have lived their lifelong ad interim, and they will be surprised to find that something they allowed to pass by unnoticed and unenjoyed was just their life— that is to say, it was the very thing in the expectation of which they lived.

The narrator of *The Wonder Years* looked back in wonder at how joyful his life was growing up, while it seemed that what he experienced at the time wasn't quite so wonderful. As Nobel Prize–winning psychologist and behavioral finance expert Daniel Kahneman has pointed out, there is often a tremendous difference between memory and experience. We often remember things very differently than we experience them. I know that this has applied to me as well.

Somehow I have carved out a pretty successful and interesting life. At one time I thought about calling this book *The Accidental Investor*, given how I stumbled onto my job and because of my very different way of thinking that seems to be better aligned with the creative, artistic types than the financial ones. A beautiful quilt has been sewn together for which, when I look back, I have fond memories. I ask myself with a sense of wonder and awe, how did this turn out the way it did? Yet in many of the moments as I was living them, I'm pretty sure it wasn't always so wonderful. If I think about what I do and to whom I'm responsible, it can be downright daunting and overwhelming at times.

My duties have entailed a great deal of responsibility toward our nearly eight hundred individual investors to ensure that the more than $1 billion they have invested with us is being managed effectively. Needless to say, I have felt a lot of pressure in my job to do well for those who have placed their trust and hard-earned capital with us. Since I am also involved in evaluating investment opportunities, I must be hypervigilant when it comes to managing risk. I am one of those people who makes decisions more on the basis of not losing versus winning. I know what you're thinking: that is not a very enjoyable way to go through life. Yet it is who I am and the way I operate. I look at the downside; I bring skepticism to the table; I try to figure out what can go wrong; and yet at the end of the day, we have to put our chips down and make our bets.

Yet, I've been doing this for over twenty-five years, so I must get something enjoyable out of it other than job and financial security. I do, but there are times I lose sight of this. I have spent many years as a married adult with two kids in private schools, mortgages, financial obligations, job pressures; I've dealt with a life-altering illness for Jacob, the death of my father, special requirements for Ariella, pressures to be more present at home; and the list goes on and on. When I focus on the responsibilities and perceived demands, I am susceptible to slipping into the "No Wonder Years." This is a modern version of Dante's *Inferno*, accompanied through hell by Virgil to see all the lost souls who lost connection with the three most important things people need: something to love, something to look forward to, and something to believe in.

There is a Jerry Garcia song called "Mission in the Rain." Robert Hunter was Garcia's lyricist and a brilliant, poetic writer. He is so gifted that Bob Dylan has asked Hunter to collaborate with him. Every time I hear the song I am infused with a sense of melancholy, since it captures so poignantly how over the course of a decade one goes from great optimism and hopes to such a sense of emptiness, despair, and pessimism. Hunter talks about a man who a decade ago was walking in the Mission District of San Francisco, and he was full of hopes and dreams. But today, he realizes that he would give anything just to have one dream at all.

This melancholy can manifest itself in a couple of ways. For those who have been fortunate enough to experience success and diverse experiences, the extraordinary can become ordinary. It just becomes harder and harder to move the wonder needle. The next dollar earned is not valued nearly as highly as it would have been in years past when money was more scarce, and the next trip is no longer anticipated with eagerness but usually with foreboding, as travel has become more of a chore. In addition, the burden of stuff— homes, cars, collectibles—and managing one's investments feels more and more like work than the stuff of dreams. In the same song, Hunter also writes, "Everything you gather is just more that you can lose."

On the other end of the spectrum are those who have never had much go their way in life, like the person in the song. They come to wonder if their luck is going to change or the demons that are controlling them can be exorcised. Will they be able to stop living paycheck to paycheck? Ironically, small, positive experiences can make a much more meaningful gain in these individuals' potential to restore some hope and optimism than those same experiences would with those who are far more well-to-do and who are much more jaded and often find very little meaning in the next dollar earned or the next experience paid for.

There's a fascinating paper titled "Money Giveth, Money Taketh Away: The Dual Effect of Wealth on Happiness" by Jordi Quoidbach, Elizabeth W. Dunn, K. V. Petrides, and Moïra Mikolajczak. They cite previous research by Dan Gilbert in his book *Stumbling on Happiness*. Gilbert identifies the *experience-stretching hypothesis* that posits that the best experiences in life can serve to diminish the more mundane, everyday joys of life. Not surprisingly, the wealthier one is, the more access one has to such extraordinary experiences. In fact, even thinking about wealth can serve to dull everyday experiences by causing them to be taken for granted. This is because scarcity seems to stimulate savoring, while abundance (actual and perceived) seems to dull it. Savoring is an emotion that can prolong and enhance positive emotional experiences. It turns out that the wealthier one is, the less savoring he or she experiences. In fact, this tends to nullify some of the other emotional benefits that wealth brings about.

Joseph Heller said, "When I grow up I want to be a little boy." Of course that's his wish because he wants to go back to a time of innocence when so much was new and fresh. Unfortunately, it is so hard to reclaim that innocence and wonder in our lives. Many of us now consistently experience restless nights, have difficulty being fully present, and are burdened by the weight of things undone. This depressing résumé provides a first-class ticket to the No Wonder Years. I think deep down that one of the reasons I wanted to write this book was to help position myself to start reclaiming wonder in my life and perhaps to help others do the same. Julia Cameron said, "Survival lies in sanity, and sanity lies in paying attention. . . . The capacity for delight is the gift of paying attention."

So what am I paying attention to in order to help reclaim wonder and awe in our lives? For those desiring to reclaim wonder, I believe the answer lies in using the resources that at the margin may no longer be wonderful as a bridge allowing others access to these resources. We actually have a volunteer program at CWS called "BRIDGE," which I will talk about later. Before doing this, however, it's important to understand what I mean by wonder and awe.

I came across a paper by Dacher Keltner and Jonathan Haidt, written in 2003, titled "Approaching Awe: A Moral, Spiritual, and Aesthetic Emotion." From their research they concluded that awe requires two attributes: perceived vastness and a need for accommodation. Accommodation is an inability to assimilate an experience into current mental structures. "Vastness refers to anything that is experienced as being much larger than the self, or the self's ordinary level of experience, or frame of reference." Such experiences can be disorienting or frightening, since they make the self feel small, powerless, and confused. They can also involve feelings of enlightenment and rebirth, when mental structures expand to accommodate truths never before known. Accommodation can be terrifying (when one fails to understand) and enlightening (when one succeeds). Think Javert and Jean Valjean from *Les Misérables*. Javert could not believe a criminal could turn good, and had to take his own life because he couldn't process this new reality. Valjean realized he had value and could be good, and dedicated his life to helping others after coming to this realization.

Campbell said the following:

> Most of us have experienced calls to the quest—great loves, passions, and losses; internal and external suffering and conflict; and opportunities to create and miscreate our own lives—but if we take them in stride without recognizing

their Soul purpose, we may be untouched by these miracles. To be transformed, we have to wake up and experience wonder. We need to ponder such events, ask to have their meaning revealed to us, and allow ourselves to recognize that we have been touched by the transpersonal world.

This requires a radical change, however, as Carl Jung pointed out to an American businessman who flew to see him to understand how he could stop drinking. Jung told him:

> Here and there, once in a while, alcoholics have had what are called vital spiritual experiences. To me these occurrences are phenomena. They appear to be in the nature of huge emotional displacements and rearrangements. Ideas, emotions, and attitudes which were once the guiding forces of the lives of these men are suddenly cast to one side, and a completely new set of conceptions and motives begin to dominate them. (*The Big Book of Alcoholics Anonymous*)

Essentially Campbell and Jung are both saying that we have to experience a powerful rewiring (a form of rebirth) if we want to break patterns that get in the way of our experiencing joy, wonder, love, and compassion. We can't get to where we want to go with the usual thought patterns and behaviors. Something powerful is often needed as a catalyst for great change.

One way of catalyzing change is to help others. It does sound cliché, but it is true from my experience and observing others. I have found that I end up keeping what I give away when I involve myself in the lives of others who can benefit by what I have to offer. One of the most valuable experiences I have had at CWS has been related to the community service program that we call BRIDGE. It was created on the premise that if the company can help support people in what they're passionate about, then the company can only benefit by having a more highly engaged, happy, and supported individual working for us. It also has the added benefit of leveraging our talent and treasure to make a difference in people's lives.

We contribute $20 per hour for up to twelve hours of volunteer work, for a total potential of $240 per year per employee. The employee can designate where 50 percent of his or her BRIDGE dollars go, while the other half goes in a company pool. Since not everyone designates where their 50 percent can go, those dollars will also go into the company pool. At the end of the year we ask participants to write a letter requesting money from the larger pool to go toward a nonprofit organization of their choice, in which they identify the organization, their involvement with the organization (if any), the reasons for their participation, and why this money will be impactful. Reading the letters is one of the highlights of my year. They are so moving and passionate, and they shine a light on so many worthy causes, many of which are far below the radar. Everyone who sends us a request will have money contributed. The range is typically $500 to $3,000. We have given away over $200,000 since the program was implemented in 1998.

Each year when we do our State of the Company meeting, going to every region to report on the year and what's ahead, we pass out the BRIDGE checks. The requirement for the recipients, however, is that they have to stand up and speak in front of the group about why they nominated the organizations for which they are receiving a check. It is so incredibly moving. Many people have been touched by family members' or personal illnesses, suicide, crime, addiction, or foster care, as well as by supporting missionary work, youth sports, and countless other worthy organizations. Tears inevitably flow, and people feel more connected when they open their hearts and souls and share openly about what they care deeply for. Henry George captured one of the best descriptions of man's yearning to make a difference for others when he said:

And, then, as the man develops his nobler nature, there arises the desire higher yet— the passion of passions, the hope of hopes—the desire that he, even he, may somehow aid in making life better and brighter, in destroying want and sin, sorrow and shame. He masters and curbs the animal; he turns his back upon the feast and renounces the place of power; he leaves it to others to accumulate wealth, to gratify pleasant tastes, to bask themselves in the warm sunshine of the brief day. He works for those he never saw and never can see; for a fame, or maybe but for a scant justice, that can only come long after the clods have rattled upon his coffin lid. . . . Amid the scoffs of the present and the sneers that stab like knives, he builds for the future; he cuts the trail that progressive humanity may hereafter broaden into a highroad.

So, I've come to the end of the road on this journey. It's been one of my life's goals (dare I say dreams?) to write a book. I am not going to let this accomplishment go by without savoring it, being proud of what I was able to achieve, and, I hope, somehow, someway, making a positive difference in the lives of some of the readers. At the end of the day, if the following were said about me, then I think I would have enjoyed a life that transformed wisdom into great wealth:

Gary Carmell was not only a loving husband and father and highly valued friend and partner, but he:

lived with purpose
thought with clarity
acted with character
grew with courage.

Works Cited

Alcoholics Anonymous, *Alcoholics Anonymous: The Story of How Many Thousands of Men and Women Have Recovered from Alcoholism (The Big Book)*, 4th Edition. New York: A.A. World Services, Inc. 2013. *http://www. aa.org/pages/en_US/alcoholics-anonymous.*

Ciardi, John (trans.). Dante Alighieri. *The Inferno.* New York: Penguin, 2001.

Allen, Frederick Lewis, *Since Yesterday: The 1930s in America.* New York: Harper Perennial, 1986.

Big Picture Blog, The. http://www.ritholtz.com/blog/

Buchanan, Mark. *Ubiquity: Why Catastrophes Happen.* New York: Broadway Books, 2002.

Campbell, Joseph. *A Joseph Campbell Companion: Reflections on the Art of Living.* Kenfield, CA: Joseph Campbell Foundation, 2011.

George, Henry. *Progress and Poverty: An Inquiry into the Cause of Industrial Depressions and of Increase of Want with Increase of Wealth: The Remedy (1879).* Boston: Adamant Media Corporation, 2002.

Gilbert, Daniel. *Stumbling on Happiness.* New York: Vintage, 2007.

Hill, Napoleon. *Think and Grow Rich.* New York: Tarcher, 2005.

Kaufman, Peter D. (ed.). *Poor Charlie's Almanack: The Wit and Wisdom of Charles T. Munger.* Marceline, MO: Walsworth, 2005.

Koo, Richard. *Balance Sheet Recession: Japan's Struggle with Uncharted Economics and its Global Implications.* Hoboken: Wiley, 2003.

Mike Norman Economics. http://mikenormaneconomics.blogspot.com/.

Mosler, Warren. *Seven Deadly Innocent Frauds of Economic Policy.* U.S. Virgin Islands: Valance Co, 2013.

Mosler, Warren. *Soft Currency Economics II.* Seattle: CreateSpace, 2013.

Naked Capitalism: Fearless Commentary on Finance, Economics, Politics and Power. www.nakedcapitalism.com.

Nickerson, William. *How I Turned $1,000 into a Million in Real Estate in My Spare Time,* rev. ed. New York: Simon & Schuster, 1969.

Yogananda, Paramahansa. *Autobiography of a Yogi.* New York: The Philosophical Library, 1946.

Schopenhauer, Arthur. *The Works of Arthur Schopenhauer.* Seattle: Editions la Bibliothèque Digitale: 2013. Kindle edition.

Shakespeare, William. *The Complete Plays of Shakespeare.* Kirkland, WA: Latus ePublishing, 2011. Kindle edition.

Sornette, Didier. *Why Stock Markets Crash: Critical Events in Complex Financial Systems* Princeton: Princeton University Press, 2004.

Soros, George. *Alchemy of Finance.* Hoboken: Wiley, 2003.

Taleb, Nassim Nicholas. *The Black Swan: The Impact of the Highly Improbable.* New York: Random House, 2007.

Woolf, Virginia. *Craftsmanship, in The Death of the Moth, and other essays.* https://ebooks.adelaide.edu.au/w/woolf/virginia/w91d/chapter24.html.

Keltner, Dacher and Haidt, Jonathan. "Approaching Awe: A Moral Spiritual and Aesthetic Emotion," *Cognition and Emotion 17*, no. 2 (2003): 297–314.

Gary Carmell is president of CWS Capital Partners, LLC, an investment management firm based in Newport Beach, California, and Austin, Texas, specializing in the acquisition, development, and management of apartment communities throughout the country, with a strong emphasis on Texas. CWS owns and operates more than twenty thousand units with an estimated value of more than $3.0 billion. Carmell joined CWS in 1987 when it was solely focused on owning, operating, and developing manufactured housing communities and had an asset base of less than $250 million. He was an integral part of the company's transition from manufactured housing to apartments, culminating in the 1998 sale of its management company and assets to a newly formed real estate investment trust backed by Security Capital Group called CWS Communities Trust.

CWS has cultivated strong bonds with its 700+ individual investors since its founding in 1969, and Carmell takes great pride and feels deep responsibility in ensuring the organization is designed in a way to generate compelling returns commensurate with an emphasis on preservation of capital. Gary has a BA in political science from UCLA, an MBA from

THE PHILOSOPHICAL INVESTOR

USC, and is a CFA charterholder. He also holds Series 22, 39, 65, and 99 FINRA licenses in connection with CWS's broker dealer, CWS Investments. He is a licensed California real estate broker and a member of the Young Presidents' Organization.

He has been married to his wife, Roneet, since 1989 and is the father of Jacob and Ariella.

INDEX

A

accommodation, 243

action, 186–87

active quality of a healthy ecosystem, 194–95

adversity
  overcoming, 182–84
  preparing for, 180–82

Alchemy of Finance, The (Soros), 21–22

American biases, 30, 148

American consumers bearing weight of world's economy, 82–84, 86–87

apartment market
  about, 185–86
  and austerity, 161
  buying opportunities, 39–40, 105–6, 111
  and CWS, 8, 29–30, 39–40, 41, 89–91, 111, 205–15
  and defense industry, 107–9
  and dot-com bubble, 57–60
  and Great Recession, 149–50
  and housing bubble, 68–69
  and housing bubble bursting, 118–19, 166–67
  lending contracted, collapsing asset values, 67–68
  Marquis at Town Centre, Broomfield, Colorado, 58–59, 62
  post-9/11, 103–5
  post-housing bubble predictions, 140–42
  rental income, 211–12
  renter nation emerging from housing bubble, 205–15
  successful purchases, 111

"Approaching Awe" (Keltner and Haidt), 243

Asian countries, 84–89, 91

Asimov, Isaac, 73

austerity, 146–47, 158, 161. *See also* savings, private sector

Autobiography of a Yogi (Yogananda), 55–56

autonomy and organization maintenance, 195–96

on delinquency rate of student
loans, 213–14
dog on a leash metaphor, 152–53
foreign custody holdings, 87
and housing bubble, 60
and interest rates, 153–54
post dot-com bubble policy, 81–82
and recovery from Great Depression, 130–31
Treasury assurance to global investors, 136
Feynman, Richard, 188
fiat currency, 151–52, 230
fingers of instability, 98
Fisher Effect, 231–32
fixed-rate loans, 56–57, 150
focus, 187–88
foreign investment in the US, 124–25,
144
fraud, 65, 67, 69, 75–76
Freddie Mac, 82–83, 117

G

George, Henry, 245–46
Gilbert, Dan, 242
global macroeconomic trends
about, 79–81
and American consumers, 82–84,
86–87
Asian countries' reserve of foreign
currencies, 85, 86–87
and China, 85–86, 91
and currencies, 88–89
and Federal Reserve policy
responses, 81
imports and exports, 86–88
Treasury assurance to global investors, 136
US dollar and Asian countries,
84–85, 86, 87–89, 91
Godley, Wayne, 148
government-aided recovery vs. private

sector recovery, 146–47, 148–49
Graham, Ben, 32
Grateful Dead, 32
gratitude and happiness, 181
Great Depression
capitalization rates, 141–42
deficits and jobs, 125–31
events leading up to, 121–23
and Federal Reserve, 130–31
and investment bubbles, 119, 122–
23, 136–38
learning from, 6, 31–32
reaction functions in 1930s compared to now, 144–48, 154–56,
162
Reconstruction Finance Corporation, 136–38
and trade deficit, 124–25
yield of riskier securities, 138–39
"Greatest Single Asset Is Seen in Real
Estate" (Jones), 137
Great Recession
about, 6–7, 116
analyzing risk to fear ratios, 138–40
and apartment market, 149–50
Great Depression reaction functions
compared to, 144–48, 154–56,
162
interest rates, 149–51
learning from newspaper articles
from 1920s and 1930s, 6
and US deficits, 148
Greenspan, Alan, 82

H

Haidt, Jonathan, 243
health and decision making, 180
"Hedge Funds Hit Rough Weather but
Stay Course" (Wall Street Journal),
100
hedging instruments, 134–35
hindsight vs. real time, 5–6

newspaper articles from earlier times, 6
New York Times, 137, 141
Nickerson, William, 39
nirvana or state of enlightenment,
13–14
noise vs. signal, 31, 34–35
nucleus metaphor, 37–38

O

Obama, Barack, 128
Occupy Wall Street movement, 159
operating principles and values, 195–96
optimism and realism, 42–43
Orange County, California, 26, 34,
105, 220
organization and autonomy maintenance, 195–96

P

painters that don't care, 40
partnership philosophy, 8, 38–39, 165.
See also marriage partnership of
Gary and Roneet
patience, virtue of, 43–44, 189–90
patterns, 10, 17–18, 29–30. *See also*
investment bubbles
perceived vastness, 243
perseverance, 182–84
personal growth, 194
personality and external validation, 238
personal unifying principal, 35
philosophical investor's philosophy
about, 172–74
and apartment market, 205–15
healthy ecosystems, 193–99
and real estate investments, 201–5
on wealth, 235–39
and wonder, 238–41, 242–46
on wonder, 238–41, 242–46
See also know thyself; partnership
philosophy; variable-rate loans
Phoenix apartment building, Purple

Sage, 41
Plant, Robert, 34–35
Plato, 56
power laws, 99
Prince, Robert, 157–58
private sector recovery vs. government-
aided recovery, 146–47, 148–49
prosperity, 100–101, 235–39
public sector payrolls, 161
Purple Sage apartment building, Phoenix, 41
purpose and dealing with adversity,
182–83
puzzles, 6, 17–18, 188, 238

Q

quiet center, operating from, 238
Quoidbach, Jordi, 242

R

rating agencies, 75–76, 134, 138
reactive vs. reflective responses, 238
reading, importance of, 20, 35
real estate, 201, 204
real estate investments
about, 15
direct control of cash flow, 205
as illiquid investments, 201–2
as inflation hedge, 204
leveragable asset class, 27, 150, 203
low volatility, 204
study of 1919–1931 market, 122
tax-deferred exchanges of real estate,
9–10, 27, 46–48, 51–53, 115–
16, 202–3
yield-oriented nature of, 203–4
See also apartment market; taxes
real estate investment trusts (REITs),
45, 49, 50, 51, 140
realism and optimism, 42–43
real time
hindsight vs., 5–6

Y

yield and risk, 138–39
yield maintenance penalties on fixed-
rate loans, 56–57
yield-oriented nature of real estate
investments, 203–4
Yogananda, Paramahansa, 55–56

Z

Zell, Sam, 207